Farid Shafiyev, Editor

Azerbaijan's Geopolitical Landscape: Contemporary Issues, 1991–2018

CHARLES UNIVERSITY
KAROLINUM PRESS

KAROLINUM PRESS
Karolinum Press is a publishing department of Charles University in Prague
Ovocný trh 3–5, 116 36 Prague 1, Czech Republic
www.karolinum.cz

© Karolinum Press, 2020
Edited by Farid Shafiyev
Texts © Shamkhal Abilov, Mitchell Belfer, Robert M. Cutler, Kamran
Ismayilov, Farid Shafiyev, Lucie Švejdová, Anar Valiyev, 2019

Cover by Jan Šerých
Graphic design by Zdeněk Ziegler
Set and printed in the Czech Republic by Karolinum Press
First edition

Cataloguing-in-Publication Data is available from the National Library
of the Czech Republic
ISBN 978-80-246-4391-5 (pb)
ISBN 978-80-246-4540-7 (pdf)

I would like to thank Mr. Eduard Gombar, Professor of Charles University, expert in Arab and Middle Eastern Studies, and former Chair of the Caspian/ Azerbaijani Centre at Charles University, who extended his support to this project.

Contents

Introduction

Farid Shafiyev

The present book is built around several major foreign policy issues faced by the Republic of Azerbaijan since it regained independence in 1991. These issues include the conflict with Armenia and related matters, the relationship with the West, the complexities of its relationship with Russia, and ties with other Muslim countries, including Iran and Saudi Arabia.

The first chapter, "The Nagorno-Karabakh Conflict: Deconstructing Stereotypes and International Imagery," is dedicated to the most acute issue for Azerbaijan's security and foreign policy: the conflict with Armenia. Taking into account recent academic publications in the English language—including Svante Cornell's edited volume[1]—which have analysed the historical, legal, and international aspects of the conflict, Shafiyev's chapter scrutinises the impact of lobby groups on the perception of the conflict in the global media, in public discourse, and among policymakers in Western countries.

Further chapters deal with Azerbaijan's relations with important regional countries and blocs. In "Rethinking Azerbaijan's Foreign Policy Strategies vis-à-vis Hegemony-Seeking Russia, 1991–2017," Kamran Ismayilov explores the dynamics of relations between Azerbaijan and Russia, the latter of which was the region's former metropole. Not long after the demise of the Soviet Union, Russia's attempts to re-establish its dominion over the South Caucasus have become evident. In this

---

1   Svante Cornell, ed., *The International Politics of the Armenian-Azerbaijani Conflict: The Original "Frozen Conflict" and European Security*, New York: Palgrave, 2017.

regard, one of the most difficult tasks for newly independent Azerbaijan in its relations with Russia was to find an appropriate foreign policy strategy that would reinforce the country's independence, sovereignty, and political autonomy. In the face of Russia's hegemony-seeking policies, Baku has responded in a way that can neither be characterised as hard balancing nor bandwagoning, as neoclassical realism would posit. Instead, Azerbaijan's foreign policy behaviour, especially since the end of 1993, has represented mixed patterns of balancing, which take indirect non-military dimesnion and cooperation towards a number of low-salience areas. In this respect, Baku conceals its true strategic intentions and counteracts Russia through less provocative means. Kamran Ismayilov unpacks the concept of "soft balancing" to both understand and explain how Azerbaijan has attempted to deal with the threatening policies of its northern neighbour. To this effect, the chapter traces Azerbaijani–Russian relations from 1991 to the present day, in order to demonstrate empirical examples of the soft balancing mechanisms employed by Azerbaijani governments.

In "Azerbaijani–EU Relations: More Opportunities on the Horizon," Anar Valiyev reviews the history of relations between Azerbaijan and the European Union. He argues that Azerbaijan aims to develop its relationship with Europe as a strategic decision, despite some obstacles presented by the different priorities of Baku and Brussels: for the former, economy and energy; and for the latter, political development. Azerbaijan attempts to pursue its own objectives within the context of this partnership, focusing on economy, energy, trade, and education. One central aspect of Azerbaijani–EU relations is the joint energy projects, namely oil and gas pipelines, from Azerbaijan to Europe. In "Azerbaijan's Place in West-Central Eurasian Energy Security," Robert Cutler underlines the importance of Azerbaijan to European energy security, giving an overview of many transregional projects involving Azerbaijan, from the 1990s through to the present day.

In the next chapter, "Azerbaijan and Turkey: Analysis of Mutual Cooperation and Strategic Relations since the Independence of Azerbaijan," Shamkhal Abilov analyses the relationship with Azerbaijan's closest ally, Turkey, in the context of the "one nation, two states" concept. He concludes that relations between the countries will remain strong through more enhanced cooperation in all spheres. The more complex relationship between Azerbaijan and Iran is explored by Mitchell Belfer in "The Next Front? Iranian Ambitions and Azerbaijan's Strategic Bulwark." According Belfer, Azerbaijan is plagued by a triple security dilemma that hems the republic into a dangerous region with aspiring geopolitical actors (notably Iran, Russia, and Turkey), brewing asymmetric challenges (growing ISIS influence in the North Caucasus and Central Asia), and a simmering dyadic conflict with an expansionist Armenia that continues to occupy Nagorno-Karabakh and adjacent regions. Given this dire security situation, Azerbaijan seems locked into a policymaking approach of strategic juggling: dealing with each challenge in part to contain, but not reduce, its impacts. Belfer, however, does not believe conditions must be this way. Azerbaijan has much more power than it currently projects, and it is capable of solving the multitude of challenges through a reassessment of its policy choices. This chapter argues that Azerbaijan needs only to comprehensively deal with one of its strategic challenges in order to solve the others; and that one challenge is Iran. Since Tehran has never reconciled itself with Azerbaijani independence, its chip-away policy has meant that it supports Armenia, assists radical Islamist elements entering Azerbaijani territory, and prevents Baku's unfettered access to Caspian gas. This work presents an assortment of strategies that may be developed by Azerbaijan to limit Iranian power and signal to its other adversaries the potential costs associated with their current policies concerning Azerbaijan. Belfer's strong criticism of Iran is not shared by some experts, who believe Azerbaijan should continue its balancing acts with regard to all regional powers.[2]

In her chapter "Emerging Strategic Partnership between Azerbaijan and Saudi Arabia: Azerbaijan's Policy of Overcoming Geography and Common Incentives," Lucie Švejdová reviews relations with another important Islamic country: Saudi Arabia. Due to its geopolitical position, alliance diversity is an essential component of Azerbaijan's foreign policy. To balance the influence of two regional powers, Russia and Iran, Azerbaijan has always sought to build a strategic partnership with allies beyond the Caucasus. This chapter analyses bilateral relations between Azerbaijan and Saudi Arabia, focusing particularly on recent developments including the expansion of cooperation in military and military-technical spheres. The mutually beneficial outcomes of strengthening strategic alliance with Saudi Arabia, particularly in the areas of security and defence, are examined in this chapter.

---

2   Marius Mazziotti, Djan Sauerborn, and Bastian Matteo Scianna, "Multipolarity is Key: Assessing Azerbaijan's Foreign Policy", *CESD Working Papers*, 2013, accessed on 7 December 2018, http://cesd.az/new/wp-content/uploads/2011/05/Paper_Multipolarity_is-key_Assessing _Azerbaijans_Foreign_Policy.pdf.

CHAPTER 1
The Nagorno-Karabakh Conflict: Deconstructing Stereotypes and International Imagery

Farid Shafiyev

Introduction

Since gaining independence from the Soviet Union in 1991, Azerbaijan has been faced with the enormous task of not only building its statehood, developing new government institutions, army, and judiciary, but also reforming its economy and replacing the Communist system with a market system. But the paramount problem faced by Azerbaijan has been its conflict with Armenia. The Azerbaijani side maintains that it faced aggression from Armenia, which resulted in the occupation of its territory in Nagorno-Karabakh and seven adjacent regions. Armenia claims that the conflict is between the central government in Baku and the Armenian population of Nagorno-Karabakh.

As much as the Armenian–Azerbaijani conflict was a real battle, it also represented a fight for international support, as each side attempted to project an image of the conflict that cast it in a favourable light (as a victim against an aggressor). In this regard, the Armenians had many advantages when the conflict erupted in 1988, as its well-established Christian diaspora had strong ties with foreign governments and citizens. This helped to garner the support of the mass media and certain public advocates, as well as securing direct military and financial contributions from both regional and global players—such as Russia and the United States—once the conflict became international, following the collapse of the Soviet Union. While ordinary Azerbaijanis complain that the West is sympathetic to Armenia due to a common religion, American and European experts tend to blame Azerbaijan's poor human rights record for its negative international image. Some experts believe that the claim that Armenian lobbyists influenced the dissemination of this narrative about Azerbaijani has been blown out of proportion.[3] This chapter seeks to disapprove this assumption.

Five Factors behind Armenian Image-Making in the Ethnic Conflict with Azerbaijan

In 1992, the US Congress imposed sanctions on Azerbaijan through the notorious Section 907 of the Freedom Support Act. At that time, Azerbaijan was ruled by President Abulfaz Elchibey, who was generally favoured by the West for his pro-democratic and pro-Western stance. Despite this, Azerbaijan was the only post-Soviet country that was punished by American sanctions. Section 907 was lobbied for by the Armenian-American community, which was "well positioned to influence US foreign policy."[4] One of the authors of Section 907 was Senator John Kerry, a highly influential politician who became secretary of state during the second Obama administration. During the 2004 presidential election, Kerry advocated for "throwing Azerbaijan under a bus."[5]

During the course of the debate on Section 907, Armenia's own military offences and human rights abuses—including the extermination of the entire Azerbaijani population in Khojaly, the largest massacre in the conflict—were not mentioned in the US Congress. American scholar Thomas Ambrosio, describing the situation of the Armenian–Azerbaijani conflict in the beginning of the 1990s, referred to "a highly permissive or tolerant international environment" which allowed the Armenian "annexation of some fifteen percent of Azerbaijani territories."[6] Armenia

---

3   Sergey Rumentsev, "Long Live Azerbaijani Diaspora!", *OpenDemocracy*, 18 May 2017, accessed on 07.02.2019, https://www.opendemocracy.net/od-russia/sergey-rumyantsev/long -live-azerbaijani-diaspora.

4   David King and Miles Pomper, "The U.S. Congress and the Contingent Influence of Diaspora Lobbies: Lessons from U.S. Policy Toward Armenia and Azerbaijan", *Journal of Armenian Studies*, 8 (1), 2004: 79.

5   David Seagal, "Time to Hit The Brakes On That Cliché", *Washington Post*, 1 May 2008, accessed 01.06.2018, http://www.washingtonpost.com/wp-dyn/content/article/2008/04/30 /AR2008043003607.html.

6   Thomas Ambrosio, *Irredentism: Ethnic Conflict and International Politics,* Connecticut: Praeger Publisher, 2001, 146.

received strong military support from Russia,[7] and was one of the biggest recipients of US aid per capita among post-Soviet states.[8]

Thus, the claim concerning the influence of the Armenian lobby should be taken seriously when dealing with the Armenian–Azerbaijani conflict. If the human rights record of Azerbaijan is the issue, then two questions should be posed:

1) Why did the United States punish Azerbaijan during President Elchibey's rule?

2) Why was Azerbaijan singled out in the Freedom Support Act while many other post-Soviet countries, including Armenia, had significant problems with human rights in the immediate aftermath of the break-up of the Soviet Union?

These questions open up the complex matter of the stereotypes and geopolitical games that have evolved in regard to Azerbaijan and have helped Armenia to garner sympathy in the West. There are five factors that advanced the Armenian annexation in the media and on the real battlefield.

1: Religion

The first factor is religion, which had a huge influence on the perception of the conflict in the eyes of Westerners. Armenian leaders used every opportunity to position the country as a "Christian outpost" surrounded by hostile Muslim states. The reality is that since its independence in 1991, Armenia enjoys good relations with Iran.[9] Armenia even helped Iranians to cope with American sanctions, by offering them western

---

7   Armenian-Russian relations are shaped by centuries-long geopolitical interests of Russian Empire, though Russia supplied weapons to both sides of the conflict since 1992. See Svante Cornell, *Small Nations and Great Powers: A Study of Ethnopolitical Conflict in the Caucasus,* Richmond: Curzon Caucasus World, 2001; Stepan Danielyan and Knar Babayan, "Nagorno-Karabakh; the Edge of Russia's Orbit", *European Council on Foreign Relations,* September 2016, accessed 01.06.2018, http://www.ecfr.eu/article/essay_nagorno_karabakh_the _edge_of_russias_orbit; Gaidz Minassian, "A Russian Outpost in the Caucasus?", *Russia/NIS Centre,* February 2008; Farid Shafiyev, *Resettling the Borderland: State Relocations and Ethnic Conflict in the South Caucasus,* Montreal: McGill-Queen's University Press, 2018.

8   Stephen M.Saideman and R. William Ayres, *For Kin or Country: Xenophobia, Nationalism, and War,* New York: Columbia University Press, 2008, 88.

9   Andrew C. Kuchins, Jeffrey Mankoff, Oliver Backes, "Armenia in a Reconnecting Eurasia: Foreign Economic and Security Interests", *Report of Centre for Strategic and International Studies,* Washington, 2016, 11-12.

banking services,[10] while Armenian ambassador Armen Navasardyan has suggested that the country, as well as the surrounding region, will benefit from Iran's nuclear weapons programme.[11] Armenia's relations with Iran are multifaceted and friendly; the two countries have even found common ground in acting against Azerbaijan, although politically, Iran has always supported Azerbaijan's sovereignty over the Nagorno-Karabakh region.[12] Thanks again to its diaspora, Armenia also has good relations with Lebanon, Syria, and Egypt.

The Armenian political narrative has emphasised the myth of the first Christian state (though it is claimed that it was not Armenia that first adopted Christianity in AD 301, but rather Osroene (Edessa), in AD 201[13]); its survival in Muslim and Turkish regions through the centuries; and the current struggle to maintain its identity. In the nineteenth and twentieth centuries, Europe's great powers exhibited a mixture of humanitarian sentiment and strategic interest in Armenia as an outpost of Christianity within the Ottoman Empire.[14] The idea of a "surviving Christian outpost"[15] became quite attractive and was well-received by various politically-active Christian groups in the West. This can be seen with Christian Solidarity Worldwide, whose once active leader, British Baroness Caroline Cox, deputy speaker of the House of Lords from 1985 to 2005, lobbied strongly on behalf of Armenia in its conflict with Azerbaijan. Thomas de

---

10   Louis Charbanneau, "Exclusive: Iran Looks to Armenia to Skirt Bank Sanctions", *Reuters*, 21 August 2012; Justin Vela, "Iran May Look North to Skirt US Sanctions, *The National: UAE Edition*, 25 November 2012.

11   Marianna Mkrtchyan, "Armenian Diplomat: Armenia Will Get Benefit from Iran's possession of Nuclear Weapons", *Arminfo*, 10 January 2018, accessed 12.02.2018, http://arminfo.info/full_news.php?id=28862&lang=3.

12   Claude Moniquet and William Racimora (eds.), "The Armenian-Iran Relationship: Strategic Implications for Security in the South Caucasus Region", *European Strategic Intelligence and Security Centre*, 13 January 2013; Robert Krikorian and Joseph Masih, *Armenia At the Crossroads*, Florence: Taylor and Francis, 2013, 117-119; Harout Harry Semerdjian, "Christian Armenia and Islamic Iran: An Unusual Partnership Explained", *The Hill*, 14 January 2013, accessed 12.04.2018, http://thehill.com/blogs/congress-blog/foreign-policy/276961-christian-armenia-and-islamic-iran-an-unusual-partnership-explained; Fareed Shafee, "Inspired from Abroad: the External Sources of Separatism in Azerbaijan, *Caucasian Review of International Affairs,* 2 (4), 2008: 205-206; Svante Cornell, *Azerbaijan Since Independence,* Hoboken: Taylor and Francis, 2015, 328-330.

13   Cheetham Samuel, *A History of the Christian Church During the First Six Centuries*, London: Macmillan and Co, 1905, 58; Charles George Herbermann, *The Catholic Encyclopedia,* New-York: Encyclopedia Press, 1913, 282.

14   Ronald Grigor Suny, '*They Can Live In The Desert But Nowhere Else': A History of The Armenian Genocide*, Princeton and Oxford: Princeton University Press, 2015, 91.

15   See the photography book by Ardillier-Carras Francoise and Balabanian Olivier, *L'Arménie : Avant-Poste Chrétien Dans Le Caucase*, Grenoble: Ed. Glenat, 2003, highlighting the country as Christian outpost.

Waal, expert in the Caucasus, has termed Armenia "an eccentric outpost of Christianity," dreaming of the recreation of Great Armenia.[16]

Azerbaijan, on the other hand, tried to obtain support from Muslim countries, especially through the Organisation of Islamic Cooperation (OIC). Yet formal support from the OIC and major Islamic countries had little impact on a global media shaped by the West. Besides, countries such as Iran, Syria, and Lebanon, with a significant Armenian diaspora, were not eager to support Azerbaijan.

2: Liberal Mantle

Secondly, Armenia was successful in presenting the irredentist movement, aimed at reclaiming territory in Nagorno-Karabakh, as a self-determinist drive with a liberal undertone. During the first years of the current conflict, Armenian nationalists spoke about the "unification" (*miatsum* in Armenian) of Armenia and Nagorno-Karabakh. In December 1989, the Armenian Soviet of Deputies (its parliament) passed a resolution to unite the region—a decision that was annulled by the Supreme Soviet of Deputies (the USSR's parliament) as illegal.[17] Yerevan failed to persuade Moscow to allow it to take the territory from Azerbaijan, and after the collapse of the USSR, tactics changed and Armenian nationalists pressed for self-determination for their brethren in Nagorno-Karabakh. This move was aimed at garnering more sympathy from liberals in the Soviet Union and around the world. The reality on the ground was different from the "liberal movement." Renowned Western scholar and Middle East expert Robert Fisk stressed in an article in *The Independent* that Armenian fighters were criminals who were slaughtering Azerbaijani civilians.[18] Human Rights Watch has reported that the killings in Khojaly, committed by Armenian troops in February 1992, were "the largest massacre to date in the conflict."[19] Johanna Popjanevski has claimed

---

16   Thomas de Waal, "An Eccentric Outpost of Christianity", *The Moscow Times*, 15 November 1997, accessed 05.05.2018, http://old.themoscowtimes.com/news/article/tmt/297472.html.
17   Edmund Herzig, *The New Caucasus: Armenia, Azerbaijan and Georgia*, London: The Royal Institute of International Affairs, Chatham House Papers, 1999, 66; International Crisis Group (ICG), "Nagorno Karabakh: A Plan for Peace", Europe Report, No. 167, 11 October 2005, 4.
18   Robert Fisk, "Echoes of Stalinism Abound in the Very Modern Azerbaijan-Armenia Conflict", *Independent,* 9 April 2016, accessed 21.05.2018, http://www.independent.co.uk/voices/echoes-of-stalinism-abound-in-the-very-modern-azerbaijan-armenia-conflict-a6976421.html.
19   "Azerbaijan: Seven Years of the Conflict", *Human Rights Watch*, 1994, accessed 07.05.2018, https://www.hrw.org/reports/pdfs/a/azerbjn/azerbaij94d.pdf.

that "the ethnic groups on both sides have been exposed to war crimes that are attributable to both parties in the conflict. As such, the current [Armenian] population of Nagorno-Karabakh can hardly be said to meet the threshold for being regarded as oppressed from the viewpoint of international law and standards."[20] The conflict produced civilian victims on both sides (although disproportionately high numbers of those killed and forced to become refugees were from Azerbaijan), but Western media paid much more attention to those on the Armenian side.[21]

At the beginning of the conflict, in 1988, Western politicians saw the separation of one autonomous entity from a Soviet republic as a sign of transformation—so fashionable during *perestroika*—a "wind of change." Moreover, for some policymakers, it was an opportunity to demand the dismantling of the Soviet Union or at least the secession of the Baltic republics from Moscow. The demand to recognise the Nagorno-Karabakh region as part of Armenia had already been supported by many Soviet liberals, such as Andrei Sakharov (whose wife Elena Bonner was an ethnic Armenian). The BBC has observed that the revision of the Soviet borders threatened the very existence of the USSR, which is why the Communist authorities supported Azerbaijan while liberals supported Armenia.[22] However, this division reflected neither the nature of the conflict nor its legal and moral dilemmas. As Robert Donaldson and Nogee Armonk stress, the Armenian–Azerbaijani conflict was both an interstate war and a war of secession. "As the aggressor in the war against Azerbaijan, Armenia felt international pressure," in the view of the UN Security Council's resolutions, which demanded the withdrawal of Armenian troops from the occupied territories, in the belief that independence superseded the idea of unification.[23]

While the West unequivocally supports the resolution of the conflicts in Georgia, Moldova, and Ukraine—on the basis of their territorial integrity—it has suggested a slightly different approach for the

20 Johanna Popjanevski, "International Law and the Nagorno-Karabakh Conflict", in *The International Politics of the Armenian-Azerbaijani Conflict*, edited by Svante Cornell, New York: Palgrave Macmillan, 2017, 27.

21 Farid Shafiyev, "Liberal Hypocrisy on Post-Soviet Separatism", *The National Interest*, 13 June 2016, accessed 30.10.2019, https://nationalinterest.org/feature/liberal-hypocrisy-post-soviet-separatism-16575.

22 "Cherniy sad: kak nachinalsa raspad SSSR", *BBC*, 11 February 2013, accessed 02.06.2018, http://www.bbc.com/russian/russia/2013/02/130131_karabakh_history.shtml.

23 Robert H. Donaldson and Nogee Joseph L. Armonk, *The Foreign Policy of Russia: Changing Systems, Enduring Interests,* New-York: M.E. Sharpe, 1998, 190.

Armenian–Azerbaijani case[24]. The West calls for a resolution based on a so-called "negotiated solution," that implies the possible secession of occupied Nagorno-Karabakh from Azerbaijan. The high number of casualties among conscripts of the Republic of Armenia during the military clashes of 2–5 April 2016 attests to the fact that Armenia is the major occupying power in the territory of Azerbaijan. Yet, that year, many Western news agencies tended to report clashes between Azerbaijan and so-called Nagorno-Karabakh forces, while in 1992–1993, a number of international news agencies reported on the war between Armenia and Azerbaijan.[25] This change confirms the success of the Armenian propaganda campaign to present the inter-state conflict as a local dispute within Azerbaijan.

In 1993, the UN Security Council (UNSC), responding to Armenian offensive attacks in Azerbaijan, adopted four resolutions. However, under pressure from Russia and France, it avoided identifying Yerevan as the main actor in this military conflict. Despite a call from one UNSC member "to call spade a spade,"[26] countries with veto power imposed their own language in draft resolutions, which avoided naming Armenia as an aggressor. Yet, the resolutions defined the Azerbaijani territories as "occupied"—a term used in international conflicts, compared to the term "controlled," which is used in internal conflicts such as in Abkhazia or Georgia. Certain elements of the UNSC resolutions point to Armenia as the active agent in the conflict. Thus, UNSC resolutions 822, 853, 874, and 884 were adopted in reaction to the occupation of Azerbaijani territories; they expressed concern about the deterioration of relations between Azerbaijan and Armenia, and urged the latter to exert influence on local Armenian forces to comply with UNSC resolutions.[27] More importantly, the UNSC reaffirmed the sovereignty of Azerbaijan over the Nagorno-Karabakh region and condemned the use of force for the acquisition of territories.

---

24 Shafiyev, "Liberal Hypocrisy on Post-Soviet Separatism".
25 Kamala Imranli-Lowe, "The Armenia-Azerbaijan Conflict Through the Prism of the British Media and the New York Times, 1988-1994", *Caucasus Survey*, 3 (2), 2015: 150-169.
26 Provisional Verbatim Record of the Statements of the Members of the Security Council, made at the 3205th meeting of the Security Council, U.N. Doc. S/PV.3205, 30 April 1993, 11.
27 UNSC resolutions are available on a number of internet resources, for example at https://2001-2009.state.gov/p/eur/rls/or/13508.htm. Good overview of the resolution done in Rovshan Sadigbayli, "The Implications of the 1993 U.N. Security Council Action for the Settlement of the Armenia-Azerbaijan Conflict", *Caucasian Review of International Affairs*, 3 (4), 2009: 342-370.

The dichotomy between the letters of international law and the opinions of some Western liberal advocates regarding a solution to the Nagorno-Karabakh problem resulted in disenchantment with the West among a certain stratum of the Azerbaijani population, and in particular, with the region's reputation as a guardian of liberal ideas and justice. A similar phenomenon can be observed in the Middle East, due to the continuing Arab–Israeli conflict. In relation to Azerbaijan, critics of the government sometimes happened to be in the pro-Armenian camp.[28] As such, their criticism of Azerbaijan's human rights record, while ignoring the situation in Armenia, comes in one package—the joint advocacy for improved human rights in Azerbaijan and the secession of Nagorno-Karabakh from Azerbaijan. This seriously damages the possible influence of so-called Westerners versus pro-Russian or Islamist forces within Azerbaijan.

3: History-Making

Third, in the interests of attracting liberal-minded politicians in the West, Armenian nationalists at home and in diaspora developed quite a distorted narrative about the historical roots of the conflict. For example, the crucial point in many Western accounts of the conflict is that Soviet leader Josef Stalin assigned Nagorno-Karabakh to Soviet Azerbaijan against the will of its Armenian majority. Highlighting the role of the vicious dictator was aimed at demonising the whole territorial arrangement allegedly made in favour of Azerbaijan against Armenia. This is a propaganda trick that is far from reality, as attested by archival documents. The brief history of the infamous decision of 1921 is as follows.

In 1918–1920, both Armenia and Azerbaijan existed as independent countries after the collapse of the Russian Empire. Their experience as independent states was shaped by the First World War, internal instability, and mutual conflict over three regions: Karabakh, Nakhichevan, and Zangezur (today's Armenian province of Sunik). British troops who occupied Azerbaijan in 1919 vested power in Karabakh to the Azerbaijani

---

28 The list includes a number of past and present Democratic US senators and congressmen (mostly with heavy Armenian constituencies such as California, New Jersey and Massachusetts) – Adam Schiff, Frank Pallone, Nancy Pelosi, Robert Menendez, etc.; Canadian Liberal Jim Karagiannis; European MPs Jaromir Stetina (Czechia), Frank Engel (Luxemborug), Eleni Theocharus (Cyprus) and some others.

general Khosrov Sultanov,[29] and the local Armenian population temporarily agreed to his rule. On 3 June 1921, after the Bolshevik takeover, the region of the South Caucasus, the Soviet Caucasian Bureau, and the governing body of the Communist Caucasus, transferred Zangezur to Armenian jurisdiction.[30] On 4 July 1921, the members of the Bureau, including Stalin, gathered in Tbilisi to discuss the issue of the mountainous area of Karabakh. Their decision, by four votes to three, was to "include" (*vklyuchit*) Karabakh in Armenia. After an objection from the Azerbaijani side, the next day the Bureau reversed its decision and decreed to "leave" *(ostavit)* Nagorno-Karabakh within Soviet Azerbaijan.[31] The language of the document speaks for itself: Nagorno-Karabakh, as an entity that already belonged to Azerbaijan, should remain under its jurisdiction. As for Stalin, even in the Caucasus in 1921, he was not an authoritative or uncontested leader; that would not be the case until the end of the 1920s. The Armenian narrative, explaining the so-called transfer of Nagorno-Karabakh to Azerbaijan only "by the will of the dictator Stalin," constitutes an attempt to find favour with the international community.

Similarly, the narrative of constant oppression suffered by the Armenians at the hands of the Turks (both Anatolian and Azerbaijani), and the ancient Armenian presence in Karabakh, are not accurate depictions based on the available historical records. Despite the fact that the first clashes between Armenians and Azerbaijanis occurred at the beginning of the twentieth century, we find hardly any animosity between Turks and Armenians in earlier history[32]. Many historical myths have been manufactured by groups of jingoists and then successfully exploited by public leaders, especially when Armenian scholars and dissidents began the Karabakh campaign in 1987–1988. In his award-winning book, *Modern Hatreds: The Symbolic Politics of Ethnic War*, Stuart Kaufman stresses that modern Armenian history developed around an idea of a martyred

---

29 Christopher J. Walker, *Armenia: The Survival of a Nation*, New York: St. Martin's Press, 1990, 270.

30 RGASPI, f. 64, op. 1, d.1, 76–7.

31 More detailed account of this issue with archival references in Jamil Gasanly, "Nagorniy Karabakh: stariyi zabluzhdeniya v novoy interpretatsiyi", *Caucasus and Globalization*, vol. 5, no. 3-4 (2011): 120-147.

32 Farid Shafiyev, "Ethnic Myths and Perceptions as a Hurdle to Conflict Settlement: The Armenian-Azerbaijani Case", *The Caucasus & Globalization Journal of Social, Political and Economic Studies*, Vol. 1 (2), 2007, 60.

Christian nation under Muslim oppression.[33] Among Azerbaijanis, there was a strong belief that Armenians were agents of the Russian Empire; as they were forced to cede Zangezur to the Armenians and then a part of the Kazakh province during Soviet rule, the Azerbaijanis feared that the Armenian claim would eventually lead to the destruction of their republic.[34]

In January 2003, Armenian president Robert Kocharian made a remark about "the ethnic incompatibility" of the Azerbaijani and Armenian people during his election campaign, implying long-standing enmity between the two.[35] This statement was condemned by the secretary general of the Council of Europe, Walter Schwimmer, as recalling the dark pages of European history.[36] Were Turks/Azerbaijanis and Armenians "ethnically incompatible" in the fifteenth, sixteenth, or eighteenth centuries? History proves that they were not—here are a few examples: a medieval Armenian chronicler, Kirakos Gandzaketsi, wrote about the leadership of one of the first Turkic Seljuk sultans of the eleventh century, Melik Shah, who absolved the Armenian priesthood from having to pay taxes[37]; Gandzaketsi wrote that "he tamed the universe, not by violence, but through love and peace"[38]; Shah Ismail Hatai, leader of the Turkic tribe Kizilbash and founder of the Safavids dynasty, which ruled over Azerbaijan, Afghanistan, and Iran from the sixteenth to the eighteenth centuries, gave Armenian traders the exclusive rights over silk; there is a popular folk song in Azerbaijan entitled *Asli ve Kerim*, about the love between a Turkic man and an Armenian woman; Sayat Nova, the famous Armenian poet, wrote many of his romantic verses in the Azerbaijani/Turkic language.[39]

Thomas de Waal, in his book *Black Garden*, highlighted friendly interactions between Azerbaijanis and Armenians before and during the conflict.[40] He writes that "the Nagorno-Karabakh conflict makes sense only if we acknowledge that hundreds of thousands of Armenians and

---

33 Stuart Kaufman, *Modern Hatreds: The Symbolic Politics of Ethnic War,* Ithaca: Cornell University Press, 2001, 53.
34 Kaufman, *Modern Hatred*, 57.
35 Shafiyev, "Ethnic Myths and Perceptions", 61.
36 Council of Europe Press Information, 30 January 2003.
37 Shafiyev, "Ethnic Myths and Perceptions", 61.
38 Kirakos Gandzaketsi, *Istoriya Armeniyi*, Moscow, 1991, 89.
39 More on history of interaction: Suleyman Mamedov's PhD dissertation, "Friendship between Azerbaijani and Armenian people", written in 1985.
40 Thomas De Waal, *Black Garden Armenia and Azerbaijan Through Peace and War*, New York: New York University Press, 2003.

Azerbaijanis were driven to act by passionately held ideas about history, identity, and rights."[41] Stuart Kaufman draws similar conclusions. Neither economic problems (Armenians rejected a package of economic benefits offered by the Soviet authorities at the beginning of the conflict) nor insecurity (the USSR was a stable country whose disappearance created a power vacuum) caused violence and subsequent war.[42] "Prejudice, fear, and a hostile myth-symbol complex can create a contest for dominance and an interethnic security dilemma," writes Kaufman.[43] Armenian ethnic identity, with an emphasis on its ancient history and genocide, collided with the Azerbaijani one, which was focused on its territory and statehood. According to Kaufman, "what made the situation so fiendishly hard to manage was not the existence of ethnic minorities, or even the tragic history of the two groups, but the way that historical myths and hostile attitudes led them to insist on mutually exclusive political goals."[44]

4: Victimhood Image

Here we are approaching the fourth element of the Armenian campaign for territorial advancement: its victimhood. Before the conflict in 1988, for decades the Armenian diaspora had been campaigning in the West for recognition of the 1915 Armenian deportation in the Ottoman Empire as "genocide." Armenian paramilitary organisations such as ASALA even coordinated a series of terrorist acts against Turkish diplomats in the 1970 and 1980s. As a result, the public in the West already viewed Armenians as "victims" of the Turks, and Azerbaijanis, as a Turkic ethnic group, were portrayed in the Armenian narrative as another "genocidal" group.[45]

In the context of decades of anti-Turkish and anti-Azerbaijani propaganda, which began much earlier than 1988, ordinary Armenians had legitimate grounds to worry about their safety and security once violence was sparked in Sumgayit in February 1988 and clashes and murders subsequently followed. However, they were caught in the nationalist narrative perpetuated by a small group of politicians, jingoists, and ethnic

---

41 De Waal, *Black Garden*, 272.
42 Shafiyev, "Ethnic Myths and Perceptions", 62.
43 Kaufman, *Modern Hatred*, 82-83.
44 Kaufman, *Modern Hatred*, 206.
45 Phil Gamaghelyan, "Rethinking the Nagorno-Karabakh Conflict: Identity, Politics, Scholarship", *International Negotiation*, 15 (1), 2010: 33-56.

entrepreneurs, while a close examination of the history of the conflict shows that violence on many occasions began with the Armenians.

The modern conflict, which "officially" began on 13 February 1988 with the Armenian protest in Nagorno-Karabakh's capital Khankendi (Stepanakert during Soviet times), was preceded by the expulsion of the Azerbaijani population in Armenia, especially in the Kafan region. This little documented event caused an influx of Azerbaijani refugees to Sumgayit and other regions of Azerbaijan. Thomas de Waal attests that intercommunal tension began in November 1987 in the Kafan and Megri regions of Armenia, which resulted in the expulsion of many Azerbaijanis.[46] During this period, several notable Armenians, such as Abel Aganbegyan, a chief economic adviser to Soviet leader Mikhail Gorbachev, expressed opinions about the transfer of Nagorno-Karabakh from Azerbaijan to Armenia: it started a "war of words."[47]

On 22 February 1988, the first clash between Azerbaijanis and Armenians occurred, which resulted in the deaths of two young Azerbaijanis.[48] The news of these first two Azerbaijani victims of the conflict inspired anti-Armenian violence in the Azerbaijani city of Sumgayit in late February 1988, which by that time was filled with refugees. On the threshold of the riot in Sumgayit, "the USSR's Deputy Procurator General A. Katusev, speaking on central TV on 27 February, told the audience about the killing of two young Azeris, specifically naming the nationality of those killed. This announcement may have acted as a catalyst."[49] Two ethnic Armenians, Eduard Grigoryan and Zhirayr Azizbekian, subsequently took part in Armenian pogroms, along with Azerbaijani criminals.

In the aftermath, many more violent clashes occurred. In 1992, as the two states became independent, a full-scale war drew both ethnic groups into the bloodshed. Both developed their own history of victimhood with the classic "blame the other" approach. Up until the mid-1990s, the Armenian narrative dominated the global media. However, Azerbaijan then also invested in an information campaign, and many journalists and

---

46 De Waal, *Black Garden,* 18-19.
47 Interview with French newspaper "L'Humanite". See also Shalala Mammadova, 'Creating the "Enemy Nation': The Difficult Historical Legacies of Armenian–Azerbaijani Relations", *Caucasus Analytical Digest,* No. 84, 14 June 2016, 9.
48 De Waal, *Black Garden*, 15; Patrick Brogan, *World Conflicts*, London: Bloomsbury Publishing, 1998, 399.
49 Alexei Zverev, "Ethnic Conflicts in the Caucasus 1988-1994", in *Contested Borders in the Caucasus*, edited by Bruno Coppieters, Brussels: VUB University Press, 1996, accessed 09.08.2017, http://poli.vub.ac.be/publi/ContBorders/eng/ch0102.htm.

experts began questioning the one-sided story. The Azerbaijani side was more successful with international organisations such as the Council of Europe and the European Parliament, which reaffirmed the territorial integrity of Azerbaijan and denounced the acquisition of territories by force.[50] The annexation of Crimea by Russia also brought more sympathy to Azerbaijan, which denounced it, while Armenia supported Moscow.

5: Armenian Diaspora

Finally, the fifth element behind the greater prominence of the Armenian narrative in the international media is its diaspora. It is estimated that about half a million Armenians each live in the United States[51] and France,[52] with a further two and a half million in Russia.[53] This well-established diaspora, including celebrities such as Charles Aznavour and Kim Kardashian, can easily deliver stories to the global media for the consumption of ordinary observers[54]. A number of Armenian public advocates and academics are available for more sophisticated readers. In general, Armenians have a longer and stronger presence in the West compared to the young and inexperienced Azerbaijanis. Baku's lobbying effort, dubbed "caviar diplomacy," has been rejected by Western liberals as the governmental efforts of an oil power[55]. While the American media has picked up that story, it completely ignores the millions spent by California's powerful Armenian community to elect favourable officials. As American scholars John Mearsheimer and Stephen Walt point out, "the disproportionate influence of small but focused interest groups increases even more when opposing groups are weak or nonexistent, because politicians have to accommodate only one set of interests and the public is likely to hear only one side of the story."[56] But the problem

---

50 See for example paragraph 2 of the Council of Europe Resolution 1416: "The Conflict Over the Nagorno-Karabakh Region Dealt With by the OSCE Minsk Conference", 2005, accessed 30.01.2018, http://assembly.coe.int/nw/xml/XRef/Xref-XML2HTML-en.asp?fileid =17289&lang=en.
51 American Community Survey, https://archive.org/details/2011AmericanCommunitySurvey Ancestry.
52 "French Senate Eyes Genocide Bill; Turkey Bristles", AP, 23.01.2012.
53 Ria Novosti, https://ria.ru/20021216/282886.html.
54 Shafiyev, "Liberal Hypocrisy on Post-Soviet Separatism".
55 Ibid.
56 John Mearsheimer and Stephen Walt, *The Israel Lobby and U.S. Foreign Policy,* New York: Farrar, Straus and Giroux, 2007, 140.

is that "lobbies do not always espouse smart policies from an American [or another host country's] viewpoint." Many groups tend to promote policies that benefit their home nation with "little regard for America-'s best interests."[57]

The irony of the Armenian diaspora's "success" in the standoff with Azerbaijan and their tremendous efforts to help the homeland is that while Nagorno-Karabakh and other Azerbaijani territories remain under Armenian control, more Armenians left the homeland and joined the diaspora. The demographic decline is alarming: almost one million Armenians have left Armenia since independence.[58] The Armenian economy is heavily dependent on transfers from expats and even more on Russian support, which comes at a high cost: Moscow controls the country's key industries and even its foreign policy.[59] Armenia is left outside of many regional projects which benefit its neighbours, such as Georgia. The reason behind the Armenian economic calamity is the country's own nationalism, propelled by the idea of a "Greater Armenia," which has drawn ethnic groups who previously lived side by side for centuries into bloody wars. This was partly caused by the failure of the first democratic republics of Armenia and Azerbaijan in 1918–1920, which became embroiled in a mutual war. Hovhannes Katchaznouni, the first prime minister of the independent Armenia in 1918, later observed a "childish and foolish plan": "a vast state was being organised and demanded—a Great Armenia from the Black Sea to the Mediterranean, from the mountains of Karabagh to the Arabian Desert. [From] where did that imperial, amazing demand emanate?"[60]

Armenia received significant military and financial support from Moscow – both during the conflict in 1992-1994 and for the past 25 years after the ceasfire. Yerevan become a member of the Moscow-led military

57 Stephen Blank, "US in the Caucasus: Beat the Russians at Their Own Game", *The Hill*, 28 January 2018, accessed 15.02.2018, http://thehill.com/opinion/international/370980 -us-in-the-caucasus-beat-the-russians-at-their-own-game.

58 Thomas De Waal, "Armenia's Population Drain", *The National Interest*, 21 November 2011, http://nationalinterest.org/commentary/armenias-population-drain-6176; official figures stands at 640,000: Joshua Kucera, "Armenia: Can the Government Reverse Demographic Decline?", *Eurasianet*, 11 July 2017, accessed 17.02.2018, https://eurasianet.org/s/armenia -can-the-government-reverse-demographic-decline".

59 Armen Grigoryan, "Armenia Likely to Yield Even More of Its Sovereignty to Russia", *Jamestown Monitor*, 8 September 2017, accessed 23.03.2018, https://jamestown.org/program/armenia -likely-to-yield-even-more-of-its-sovereignty-to-russia.

60 Hovhannes Katchaznouni, *The Armenian Revolutionary Federation (Dashnagtzoutiun) Has Nothing to Do Anymore,* edited by John Roy Carlson and translated by Matthew A. Callender, New York: Armenian Information Service, 1955, 12.

Collective Security Treaty Organisation (CSTO) and the economic Eurasian Customs Union. Armenian financial institutions were a channel to the global financial market for Iranian banks during the time of sanctions.[61] Armenia, according to Wikileaks, was involved in arms trade with Iran. John D. Negroponte, the US Deputy Secretary of State at the time, wrote a December 2008 letter to Armenian president Serzh Sargsyan, expressing "deep concerns about Armenia's transfer of arms to Iran which resulted in the death and injury of US soldiers in Iraq."[62] Sargsyan came to power in 2008 through rigged elections, which resulted in the killing of ten citizens during demonstrations in March of that year. In neighbouring Azerbaijan, anything close to this scale of unlawful activity—illegal arms trade, evasion from sanctions, and murders of protesters—would have drawn strong condemnation from Western countries.

Yet, despite all this, the United States and the EU are still pandering to the "Christian outpost" on the far eastern frontier of Europe. Yerevan has successfully sold the notion of Christian solidarity "in the face of a Muslim threat" to many Christian rights activists through its influential lobby in America and Europe.

Conclusion

The situation of Armenia, given its behaviour and its status as an *enfant terrible*, makes it even more difficult to envisage the success of the results--oriented peaceful negotiations which both sides have continued to hold since 1992, under the auspices of the Minsk Group, co-chaired by France, Russia, and the United States. All three countries have strong Armenian diasporas and have historically exhibited favouritism in respect to the Armenian cause. At the same time, two of the countries, the United States and Russia, have strategic geopolitical disagreements, which makes their joint work on a solution more complicated.[63]

---

61 Louis Charboneau, "Exclusive: Iran Looks to Armenia to Skirt Bank Sanctions", *Reuters*, 21 August 2012.
62 Eli Lake, "WikiLeaks: Armenia Sent Iran Arms Used to Kill U.S. Troops", *The Washington Times*, 29 November 2010, accessed 16.05.2018, https://www.washingtontimes.com/news/2010/nov/29/wikileaks-armenia-sent-iran-arms-used-to-kill-us-t/.
63 There are a number of sources on the process of the negotiation between Armenia and Azerbaijan, and the role of international mediators. Svante Cornell, *The International Politics of the Armenian-Azerbaijani Conflict: The Original "Frozen Conflict" and European Security*, New York:

Azerbaijan also has some work to do. However, the amelioration of human rights and economic advancement—the latter improved with the flow of oil money—will not settle the countries' conflict unless Armenia also resolves the issues of its national identity—in particular, the recreation of a "Great Armenia" and a "permissive" international environment. As manifested by recent events in liberal democracies such as the United Kingdom and Spain concerning Scotland and Catalonia, respectively, it is clear that economic advantages or disadvantages are not the cause of ethnic tensions. However, compliance with European values, based on the principles of territorial integrity and minority rights, might serve as the only solution to the problem if the great powers put aside their game playing.

Armenia is not a winner from this prolonged conflict, despite its control over Nagorno-Karabakh, because it has effectively lost its sovereignty to Russia. Without friendly relations with Azerbaijan and Turkey, Yerevan's regional isolation will remain, and the prospects for economic growth will be as bleak as they have been for the past twenty-five years. Nor can Armenia's supporters in the West—both so-called liberals and conservative Christian groups—claim success, as Yerevan falls into Moscow's grip. Recent revolutions in Armenia are unlikely to alter the country's geopolitical situation. Rather, for the short term, the winner is Moscow, which effectively limits Armenia's and Azerbaijan's strategic foreign policy choices.[64]

Palgrave Macmillan, 2017; Svante E Cornell, *Azerbaijan Since Independence,* Hoboken: Taylor and Francis, 2015, 137-161; Fariz Ismailzade, *The Nagorno-Karabakh Conflict: Current Trends and Future Scenarios*, Roma: Istituto affari internazionali, 2011; Bahar Baser, *Third Party Mediation in Nagorno-Karabakh: Part of the Cure or Part of the Disease?* Saarbrücken, VDM Verlag, 2008; Moorad Mooradian & Daniel Druckman, "Hurting Stalemate or Mediation? The Conflict over Nagorno-Karabakh, 1990-95", *Journal of Peace Research*, 36 (6), 1999: 709-727.

64 Eduard Abrahamyan, 'Is Armenia Testing a New Foreign Policy Concept?", *Jamestown Monitor*, 15 (16), 1 February 2018, accessed 11.05.2018, https://jamestown.org/program/armenia -testing-new-foreign-policy-concept.

CHAPTER 2
Rethinking Azerbaijan's Foreign Policy Strategies vis-à-vis Hegemony-Seeking Russia, 1991–2017

Kamran Ismayilov

Introduction

In the early years of independence, Azerbaijan endured severe hardships, suffering from an economic crisis, political instability exacerbated by social discontent, and an international conflict involving neighbouring Armenia. Although Azerbaijan managed to overcome the economic difficulties and domestic instability that had challenged its survival in the early 1990s, Armenia's conflict with Azerbaijan remains the most serious threat to Baku's security.

The Armenian–Azerbaijani conflict was triggered when Armenians living in the Nagorno-Karabakh region of Azerbaijan took up arms, with the aim of seceding from Azerbaijan and joining Armenia. This dispute eventually turned into a full-scale war between the two countries. A ceasefire was reached in 1994, resulting in the occupation of almost twenty percent of Azerbaijan's internationally recognised territories by Armenian forces, including the mountainous Karabakh region. This caused approximately 30,000 deaths and led to an influx of hundreds of thousands of internally displaced people (IDP).[65]

The so-called Minsk Group, co-chaired by Russia, France, and the United States, was set up under the auspices of the OSCE at the organisation's Budapest Summit in 1994, and given a legal mandate to mediate

---

65 For more information on the Armenian-Azerbaijani Nagorno-Karabakh conflict, see Thomas De Waal, *Black Garden: Armenia and Azerbaijan through Peace and War*, New York: New York University Press, 2003; Svante Cornell, *The International Politics of the Armenian-Azerbaijani Conflict: The Original "Frozen Conflict" and European Security*, New York: Palgrave Macmillan, 2017.

peace negotiations over the Nagorno-Karabakh conflict.[66] However, unlike the United States and France, Russia is the main security ally of Armenia, which has enjoyed both formal and informal support from Russia since the early days of the conflict.[67] These claims were later confirmed by leaked reports, showing that Russia transferred military armaments worth $1 billion to Armenia in the early 1990s.[68]

The good nature of Armenian–Russian relations predates the Soviet era. For many years, Moscow acted as a guarantor of Armenia's sovereignty and security interests.[69] Post-Soviet Russia continues its historical security relationship with Armenia, thus retaining its crucial role in the country's security interests, which is clearly stated in the National Security Strategy of the Republic of Armenia.[70] Both are members of the Collective Security Treaty Organisation (CSTO), a Russian-led military alliance, and Russia maintains a significant military presence in the country. The second largest city in Armenia, Gyumri, some 100 kilometres from the capital Yerevan, is home to Russia's 102nd military base, where between three and five thousand Russian troops are stationed, along with tanks, fighter jets, helicopter gunships, and anti-aircraft missiles. The two countries have also established a joint air defence system, and most recently agreed to form a permanent joint ground force, by integrating the Armenian army into the Southern Military District of the Russian Armed Forces. For years, Russia has also offered financial loans to Armenia with low interest rates, so that it can acquire Russian weapons at a discount.

Russia's military alliance with Armenia can be seen as part of Moscow's post-Soviet grand strategy of re-establishing its regional leadership in its "near abroad." This strategy implies exclusivity without any power-sharing.[71] As observed by a number of commentators and analysts, in

---

66 Hungarian OSCE Chairmanship, Mandate for the Co-Chairmen of the Minsk Process, OSCE, 23 March 1995, accessed 27.08.2018, http://www.osce.org/mg/70125?download=true.

67 John P. Willerton, Gary Goertz, Michael O. Slobodchikoff, "Mistrust and Hegemony: Regional Institutional Design, the CIS, and Russia", 18 (1), 2015, 26-52.

68 Fariz Ismailzade, "Russian Arms to Armenia Could Change Azerbaijan's Foreign Policy Orientation", *Central Asia-Caucasus Analyst*, 11 (2), 2009.

69 Willerton, Goertz, Slobodchikoff, "Mistrust and Hegemony: Regional Institutional Design, the CIS, and Russia", 11.

70 Republic of Armenia, National Security Strategy of the Republic of Armenia, 2007, accessed 27.08.2018, https://www.files.ethz.ch/isn/155589/Armenia%20National%20Security%20Strategy%202007_eng.pdf.

71 Neil S. MacFarlane, "Contested Regional Leadership: Russia and Eurasia", in *Regional Powers and Contested Leadership*, Hannes Ebert, Daniel Flemes (eds.), Palgrave Macmillan, 2018, 275-299.

the post-Soviet space, Russia desires to be the only actor who has a right to interfere.[72] In the interests of achieving this goal, Moscow has used the various military, economic, and cultural tools at its disposal. In addition, Kremlin-initiated projects—such as the Commonwealth of Independent States (CIS), CSTO, and EEU—should be understood as part of this strategy. Russia has actively sought to ensure the membership of the former Soviet republics in these organisations.

Russia's approach towards Azerbaijan in the post-Soviet era is characterised by continuous attempts to exercise a predominant influence over the direction of Baku's domestic and foreign affairs. For years, Moscow has employed different tactics to pressure Baku into joining Russian-led organisations, while preventing Azerbaijan from establishing closer ties with the West or pursuing policies that would undermine Russia's geopolitical and geoeconomic interests. In doing so, Moscow has pursued its strategic goals at the expense of Azerbaijan's national interests. For example, Russia has made numerous attempts to hinder the implementation of Azerbaijani energy projects, in order to preserve its dominant position in the European energy market. Moscow has also significantly expanded its military presence in the region, especially in the Caspian Sea, and strengthened its military alliance with Armenia, notwithstanding that these actions have contributed to Azerbaijan's growing sense of insecurity. As a result, Russia's political agenda has been met with suspicion in Baku. However, the power-asymmetry between the two, coupled with Moscow's important role in the Nagorno-Karabakh peace process and some economic considerations, have constrained Azerbaijan's foreign policy choices in dealing with the threatening policies of Russia.

As this brief introduction to the regional geopolitical dynamics has shown, ever since the state declared independence in 1991, the most significant foreign policy challenge for consecutive Azerbaijani governments has been to find a strategy that would mitigate the security threats posed by Moscow's geopolitical ambitions, while also maintaining working relations with Russia in the areas that would be beneficial for Baku. This chapter traces how, as a relatively weak and small state, Azerbaijan has reacted to Russia's aim to restore its regional hegemony since the breakup of the Soviet Union. The remaining sections of this chapter begin with a theoretical framework, which will be followed by discussion

---

72   Sven Biscop, "The EU and Multilateralism in an Age of Great Powers", In *Multilateralism in a Changing World Order*, Christian Echle Patrick, Rueppel Megha Sarmah, Yeo Lay Hwee (eds.), Singapore: Konrad-Adenauer-Stiftung, 2018, 39-49.

of the various foreign policy strategies that relatively small states like Azerbaijan can employ to deal with more powerful states like Russia. The last two sections will first examine Russia's aspirations for regional leadership, and then analyse foreign policy strategies used over the years by various Azerbaijani leaders.

The Balance of Threat Theory and Strategies of Resistance and Accommodation

This chapter's theoretical point of departure is neorealism. Although there are different variants of neorealism, they all share a set of general assumptions about international politics. Neorealist scholars agree that the nature of the international system is anarchic; that states are the major international players in international relations; that international politics is a never-ending struggle among states; and that anarchy in the international system compels states to prioritise their own security without relying on any other actor.[73] Most neorealist scholars treat the structure of the international system as the only determinant of international politics. However, as noted by Stephen Walt, anarchy in international politics is not an independent causal force, but rather a permissive condition.[74]

In foreign policy behaviour, although the structure of the international (regional) system makes it possible to understand what constrains states' actions, it is not sufficient to fully understand and explain the foreign policy choices of states. In other words, as argued by Ripsman and others, the structure of the international system and structural modifiers "shape the broad parameters of possible strategies that states can pursue," but they will be conditioned by other non-material variables.[75] This chapter posits that the foreign policy behaviour of Azerbaijan between 1991–2017 could best be understood and explained through the application of Walt's "balance of threat theory."

---

73 See Kenneth Waltz, *Theory of International Relations*, Reading: Addison-Wesley, 1979.
74 Stephen M. Walt, "The Enduring Relevance of the Realist Tradition," in *Political Science: The State of the Discipline*, ed. Ira Katznelson and Helen V. Milner, New York: W. W. Norton, 2002, 211.
75 Norrin M. Ripsman, Jeffrey W. Taliaferro, and Steven E. Lobell, *Neoclassical Realist Theory of International Politics*, New York: Oxford University Pres, 2016.

Rooted in the neorealist theory of international relations, the balance of threat theory challenges the balance of power arguments that states try to build their power to match the material capabilities of the strongest state, regardless of whether the stronger state is benign or hostile. After conducting a comprehensive study analysing the foreign policy behaviour of a number of states, Walt concludes that states tend to accept the rise of nonaggressive powers while they would balance against more aggressive threats, even if they are less powerful.[76] Hence, states' behaviour is driven by a perceived threat, and not a desire to maintain a balance of power per se.[77] In other words, the balance of threat theory posits that although power distribution in the international or regional system is an important factor when states formulate a foreign policy strategy, they respond more strongly to shifts in the level of an external threat. According to Walt, the factors that affect the level of threat that states may pose are aggregate power and offensive capabilities, proximity, and aggressive intentions.[78]

The balance of threat theory posits that states will primarily either choose bandwagoning or balancing to respond to the threats. Bandwagoning means aligning with the strongest or most threatening state. It may either be defensive, with the purpose of neutralising the powerful state or avoiding conflict with it, or offensive, in order to profit by the alignment. Walt explains bandwagoning as a strategy of appeasement, where the bandwagoner opts out of resisting the dominant power and instead realigns its foreign policy in order to support it. In doing so, the bandwagoning state tries to prove itself as a loyal supporter, hoping to benefit from the powerful state or to be left alone,[79] putting its "fate in the hands of a more powerful state whom they suspect (usually with good reason) of harboring hostile intentions."[80]

Balancing, on the other hand, is a proactive strategy employed to ensure that "a more powerful state cannot use its superior capabilities in ways that the weaker side will find unpleasant."[81] Traditionally, balancing is understood as a strategy for increasing one's own military power (balancing internally) and/or joining military alliances (balancing

---

76 Stephen M. Walt, *The Origins of Alliances*, New York: Cornell University Press, 1987.
77 Walt, *The Origins of Alliances*, vi.
78 Ibid., 22.
79 Stephen Walt, *Taming American Power: The Global Responses to US Primacy,* New York: W. W. Norton, 2005.
80 Walt, *Taming American Power*, 183.
81 Ibid., 120.

externally), in order to provide protection from more powerful states. Hans Morgenthau and Kenneth Thompson define balancing as an "attempt on the part of one nation to counteract the power of another by increasing its strength to a point where it is at least equal, if not superior, to the other nation's strength."[82] However, most recently, international relations scholars have recognised that balancing is not only limited to military buildup or alliance formation.[83]

Robert Art asserts that balancing is a behaviour "designed to create a better range of outcomes for a state vis-à-vis another state or coalition of states by auditing to the power assets at its disposal, in an attempt to offset or diminish the advantages enjoyed by that other state or coalition."[84] Means of balancing include, but are not limited to: military forces, economic military power and leverage, formal alliances, informal alignments, and voting and veto power in international organisations. Based on this conceptualisation of "balancing," Art together with Robert Pape and T. V. Paul proposed a new type of balancing act—"soft balancing"—as the opposite of hard balancing.[85]

While traditional hard balancing involves military buildups and alliances, soft balancing involves primarily non-direct and non-military measures. The main aim of a country that employs soft balancing is not to challenge the military preponderance of the opponent, but to delay, frustrate, and undermine aggressive and threatening policies.[86] Paul defines soft balancing as "limited, tacit, or indirect balancing strategies largely through coalition building and diplomatic bargaining within international institutions, short of formal bilateral and multilateral military alliances."[87] As becomes clear from the definition of the concept, the mechanisms of soft balancing include: territorial denial, diplomatic coordination and entanglement, signalling of resolve to participate in

82 Hans Joachim Morgenthau and Kenneth W. Thompson, 9th ed., *Principles & Problems of International Politics: Selected Readings*, New York: Alfred A. Knopf, 1950.
83 Kai He, "Institutional Balancing and International Relations Theory: Economic Interdependence and Balance of Power Strategies in Southeast Asia", *European Journal of International Relations*, 14 (3), 2008: 489-518.
84 Robert Art, Stephen Brooks, William Wohlforth, Keir Lieber, and Gerard Alexander, "Correspondence: Striking the Balance", *International Security* 30 (3), 2006: 177–96.
85 Robert Pape, "Soft Balancing Against the United States", *International Security*, 30 (1), 2005: 7-45; Robert J. Art, "Correspondence: Striking the Balance", *International Security*, 40 (3), 2006: 177-196; Thazha V. Paul, "Soft Balancing in the Age of U.S. Primacy", *International Security*, 30 (1), 2005: 46-71.
86 Pape, "Soft Balancing Against the United States", 7.
87 Paul, "Soft Balancing in the Age of U.S. Primacy", 58.

a balancing coalition, economic statecraft,[88] developing exclusive institutions, strategic non-cooperation, and providing aid to rivals.[89]

Soft balancing is a concrete policy pursued by states under particular conditions. Paul defines the conditions that either provoke or dissuade states to engage in soft balancing as follows:

"1. The hegemon's power position and military behaviour are of growing concern but do not yet pose a serious challenge to the sovereignty of second-tier powers.
 2. The dominant state is a major source of public goods in both the economic and security areas that cannot simply be replaced.
 3. The dominant state cannot easily retaliate either because the balancing efforts of others are not overt or because they do not directly challenge its power position with military means."[90]

Soft balancing strategies involve a degree of engagement with the hostile power. As Paul points out, when pursuing soft balancing, states could engage the threatening power and "develop institutional links with it to ward off possible intense retaliatory actions." In fact, soft balancing is not a strategy that is employed exclusively against a foe or an arch-enemy, but it may very well take place "between friends."[91] However, when employed against a rival, one should not rule out the possibility of soft balancing turning into hard balancing. In fact, when the perceived level of threat rises—meaning when the threatening state becomes an imminent challenge to the security of another state—then balancing efforts will likely intensify and turn into hard balancing.

Hence, the choice between bandwagoning and balancing is largely a function of the combination of an aggregate/offensive power,

---

88 Baldwin defines economic statecraft as a strategy that involves all the economic actions through which one may influence others. David A. Baldwin, *Economic Statecraft*, Princeton: Princeton University Press, 1985.
89 See Paul, "Soft Balancing in the Age of U.S. Primacy"; Kai He and Huiyun Feng,"If Not Soft-Balancing, then What? Reconsidering Soft Balancing and U.S. Policy toward China", *Security Studies*, 17, 2008: 363-395; Judith Kelley, "Strategic Non-cooperation as Soft Balancing: Why Iraq Was Not Just about Iraq", International Politics, 42 (2), 2005: 153-173; Ilia Z. Saltzman, "Soft Balancing as Foreign Policy: Assessing American Strategy Toward Japan in the Interwar Period", *Foreign Policy Analysis*, 8 (2), 2012: 131-150.
90 Paul, "Soft Balancing in the Age of U.S. Primacy", 59.
91 Beth E. Whitaker, "Soft balancing among weak states? Evidence from Africa", *International Affairs,* 86 (5), 2010: 1109-1127; Franz Oswald, "Soft Balancing Between Friends: Transforming Transatlantic Relations", *Debate: Journal of Contemporary Central and Eastern Europe*, 14 (2), 2006: 145-160.

geography, and aggressive intentions. Although Walt does not explicitly explain when and why states choose between hard and soft balancing strategies, based on the logic of the balance of threat theory, it can be argued that the choice between hard and soft balancing is largely determined by the perception of hostile intent of the hegemon or more powerful state. Therefore, the dominant powers' intent and policies, and their perception by governments of other states, are important, as they could affect balancing in important ways. By applying the balance of threat theory to study the case of Azerbaijani–Russian relations, I argue that geography, aggregate and offensive power, and perceived aggressive intentions have largely determined Azerbaijan's reactions to Russia.

Hegemony-Aspiring Russia

In the aftermath of the dissolution of the Soviet Union, Russia suffered from a series of domestic crises that not only led to the decline in its overall capabilities but also threatened its integrity as a state. Nonetheless, Moscow remained the region's premier economic, military, and cultural power.[92] The already existent asymmetry between Russia and other post-Soviet countries in terms of military, economic, and cultural capabilities has widened particularly since Vladimir Putin assumed the presidency and managed to stabilise the internal situation in the country. After he took office, Russia's economy started to recover, which enabled Putin to invest more in the country's capacity to project power in its neighbourhood.

Today, Russia has a population of 145 million, almost equal to the combined population of all other former Soviet republics; while its GDP is almost twice that of the other post-Soviet states combined. In 2000, Russia's GDP accounted for slightly more than $260 billion, but by 2017 it had increased to $1.57 trillion.[93] In contrast, Azerbaijan's GDP totalled $5.2 billion and $40 billion in 2000 and 2017, respectively.[94] In the last decade, Russia has converted its economic growth into an increased

92 Stefan Meister, "Hedging and Wedging: Strategies to Contest Russia's Leadership in Post-Soviet Eurasia", in *Regional Powers and Contested Leadership*, Hannes Ebert, Daniel Flemes (eds.), Palgrave Macmillan, 2018, 301-326.

93 World Bank, Russian Federation, GDP (Current US$), accessed 27.08.2018, https://data .worldbank.org/indicator/NY.GDP.MKTP.CD?locations=RU.

94 World Bank, Russian Federation, GDP (Current US$), accessed 27.08.2018, https://data .worldbank.org/indicator/NY.GDP.MKTP.CD?locations=AZ.

military budget. While Russia's military expenditure in 2000 totalled $9.2 billion, in 2017 the budget reached $66.3 billion; whereas Azerbaijan spent $1.5 billion in 2017.[95] One study suggests that the Russian defence industry is one of the largest in the world, second only to the United States in terms of employment and the range of weapons systems and other military equipment it produces.[96] Russia also enjoys a significant military presence in the region. It maintains military bases and installations in a number of neighbouring countries, including Armenia, Belarus, Kazakhstan, Kyrgyzstan, and Tajikistan, as well as in some occupied territories or separatist regions, including Abkhazia, South Ossetia, Transnistria, and Crimea. Given that it possesses much greater resources (population as well as economic and military capabilities) compared to other former Soviet republics, Russian policymakers have seen their country as the regional hegemon, and have expected that the rest of the world will accept this.

Since the early 1990s, the Russian political elite has been dominated by conservatives within powerful state institutions, including the parliament and military, who see international politics as an area where major actors have to compete. Therefore, they have argued that Russia is forced to protect its military security and economic interests. For this reason, they have insisted that Russia needs to restore its status as a great power in world politics and to re-establish its "sphere of influence" in the near abroad.

The "sphere of influence" notion suggests that a dominant power enjoys special rights, responsibilities, and interests in an area outside its sovereign jurisdiction.[97] To explain it in a Russian context, the national elite sees the international system in terms of a hierarchical order, where each great power is entitled to maintain its own sphere of influence. In this respect, Russia regards its near abroad—countries of the former Soviet Union, except for the Baltic states—as an area where Moscow has privileged entitlements. Therefore, Russia seeks international recognition of its special rights and obligations in the post-Soviet region. In doing so, Russian policymakers overtly show their intentions. For instance, in the

SIPRI Military Expenditure Database, accessed 27.08.2018, https://www.sipri.org/databases/milex [Direct link not available].

95 Svante Cornell, *Azerbaijan Since Independence*, New York: Sharpe, Inc., 2011.

96 Natasha Kuhrt and Valentina Feklyunina (eds.), *Assessing Russia's Power: A Report*, Newcastle: The British International Studies Association, 2017.

97 MacFarlane, "Contested Regional Leadership: Russia and Eurasia", 279-280.

aftermath of the Russo-Georgian War in 2008, Russia's claim of a "privileged" sphere of influence in the world was crystallised when the the then President, Dmitry Medvedev, stated that in some parts of the world, Moscow wants to have a final say and it expects the world to respect that.[98] Under such circumstances, Stefan Meister rightly observes that the Russian elite sees its country as playing the role of regional hegemon, thereby limiting the sovereignty of former Soviet republics.[99] In the same vein, Neil MacFarlane asserts that the Russian elite aims to lead the newly independent states and Moscow believes it has the right to do so, whereby Russia challenges the freedom of post-Soviet states to make sovereign foreign and security policy decisions.[100]

With the aim of gathering the former Soviet republics under its leadership, Russia has pursued several strategies, including formalising and institutionalising its sphere of influence. The first step in this direction was taken in 1991, when Russia, Belarus, and Ukraine came together to launch the CIS. As envisaged in the initial documents, the CIS aims to maintain the economic space that existed in the Soviet Union and to cooperate on foreign and security issues.[101] The other organisations that have been established under Russian leadership are the CSTO and EEU; they are currently the most important components of Russia's foreign and security policy.

Russian policymakers have made it their foremost priority to expand the memberships of these organisations. Meister argues that regional organisations are used as instruments to preserve the dependencies of post-Soviet states and prevent other integration options. Similarly, Stephen Blank believes that Russia regards the regional organisations as a way to sustain its "sovereignty over that of CIS countries rather than achieving economic or military integration."[102] Thus, it can be argued that through the regional integration projects, Moscow aims to reconstitute its sphere of influence.

---

98 "Russia Claims Its Sphere of Influence in the World", *The New York Times*, August, 2008, accessed 27.08.2018, https://www.nytimes.com/2008/09/01/world/europe/01russia.html
99 Meister, "Hedging and Wedging: Strategies to Contest Russia's Leadership in Post-Soviet Eurasia", 301.
100 MacFarlane, "Contested Regional Leadership: Russia and Eurasia", 279-280.
101 Ibid., 280.
102 Stephen Blank, "The Intellectual Origins of the Eurasian Union Project", in *Putin's Grand Strategy: The Eurasian Union and its Discontents,* Fredrick Starr and Svante Cornell (eds.), Washington D.C: Central Asia-Caucasus Institute, 2014.

To achieve its objectives, Moscow has utilised its economic, political, social, and military capabilities, using them as both carrots and sticks. Russia uses coercive tactics—including economic and energy pressure (introducing embargoes on specific imports, cutting hydrocarbon supplies, increasing energy prices, for example), political pressure (such as threatening to deport migrants to their home countries), and military superiority—as a way to threaten small states that are not loyal and attempt to integrate with competing organisations. In this case, as the annexation of Crimea and the subsequent war in Eastern Ukraine have clearly demonstrated, direct military intervention is also an option.

To sum up, following the demise of the Soviet Union, Russia has sought to restore its dominant influence over the former Soviet republics, including Azerbaijan. Russia's behaviour has forced relatively small regional states to adopt strategies to respond to Russia's policies and actions. Despite facing similar structural pressures, however, the responses of these states have varied over time. This chapter argues that their responses to Russia have been conditioned by a combination of three factors: geography, aggregate and offensive power, and aggressive intentions.

Among these determinants, geography is the crucial factor to understanding any state's foreign policy behaviour. Writing on the opportunities and challenges presented to a country's foreign policy by its geography, Christopher Hill argues that "on the one hand the physical environment imposes costs and constraints. If a government tries to ignore the vulnerability of its borders, or gambles on always getting good harvests, it may be severely punished by events. On the other, the physical world provides varying kinds of opportunity."[103]

As a small country situated in a strategically critical part of the world—Azerbaijan connects the Caucasus to Central Asia, Europe to Asia, and Russia to the Middle East—its geography allows it to play the role of a bridge between east and west, north and south. Yet, the Caucasus has historically been the object of geopolitical competition between the Persian, Russian, and Ottoman empires. Although the empires are gone today, their successor states (Iran, Russia, and Turkey) continue to seek to exert influence over the regional countries' domestic and foreign

---

103 Christopher Hill, *Foreign Policy in the Twenty-first Century*, London: Palgrave Macmillan, 2016, 180.

affairs, thereby posing a challenge to their independence, sovereignty, and political autonomy.

Similarly, the aggregate and offensive power of Russia, which cannot be matched by Azerbaijan, has a significant impact on Azerbaijan's foreign policy behaviour. However, considering that geography is a constant variable, while the power asymmetry between Russia and Azerbaijan has remained the same for years, we can assume that changes both in Russia's intentions and how Azerbaijani leaders have perceived Moscow's geopolitical ambitions have had a major impact on the development of Azerbaijan's foreign policy.

Rethinking Azerbaijan's Reactions to Hegemony-Seeking Russia, 1991–2017

While Russia has seen itself as a regional hegemon that has "special rights and obligations" in the post-Soviet region, and has used its economic, political, and military power to preserve the dependencies of post-Soviet states and prevent their other integration options, Azerbaijan, since the early years of independence, has pursued foreign policy based on its own interests, that on many occasions contradict those of the Kremlin. The National Security Concept of the Republic of Azerbaijan identifies protecting the "independence and territorial integrity, ensuring inviolability of its internationally recognised borders" as the most important foreign and security policy tasks of Azerbaijan's government.[104] Accordingly, threats to Azerbaijani national security are categorised as: 1) acts against Azerbaijan's independence, sovereignty, and territorial integrity; 2) acts against the country's energy infrastructures; 3) political, military, and economic dependency on other, foreign actors; and 4) regional militarisation.[105]

Faced with the reality of Russia's increasing desire for regional domination, Azerbaijani leaders since the early years of independence have been under pressure to deploy a strategy that would best serve the country's interests. Both international and local observers who have examined Azerbaijan's reactions to Russia have mostly arrived at divergent conclusions. While some have characterised the country's foreign

---

[104] Republic of Azerbaijan, National Security Concept of the Republic of Azerbaijan, 2007, accessed 27.08.2018 https://www.files.ethz.ch/isn/154917/Azerbaijan2007.pdf.
[105] Ali Hasanov, *Azerbaydzhanin Geosiyaseti*, Baku: Zardabi LTD, 2015, 878-884.

policy towards its biggest neighbour in terms of a strategy to resist Moscow's dominance in the region through energy cooperation with the West, others have assumed that Baku "has rejected balancing altogether" in its external relations.[106] Some have looked at Baku's approach towards Russia as a continuation of the former's "balanced foreign policy"—policy that has been officially adopted by Baku. Anar Valiyev, for instance, describes Baku's foreign policy as "silent diplomacy," aimed at reinforcing its position in the region by exploiting contradictions between different international actors.[107] According to Farid Ismayilzade, the "balanced foreign policy" is calculated to lessen external pressures by manoeuvering between different power centres, in order to avoid retaliatory policies by more powerful states.[108] In the same vein, Nargiz Mehdiyeva argues that Azerbaijan has pursued "strategic maneuvering," thus avoided bandwagoning with Russia.[109] In the opinion of Kamal Makili-Aliyev, Azerbaijan's strategy towards Russia aims at transforming the potential threats into strategic partnerships and opportunities.[110] The present chapter builds on the previous studies and aims to contribute to the literature, by using a novel concept to understand Azerbaijan's foreign policy strategy more accurately.

Within the framework of balance of threat theory, this chapter subscribes to the view that states may either challenge or accommodate powerful threatening states. Traditionally, realist scholarship focuses on two extreme poles of foreign policy strategies: balancing (understood as a military buildup or joining in alliances) or bandwagoning.[111] However, as previously shown, there are "various middle-range strategies for

106 Doug Blum, "Beyond Blood and Belief: Culture, Identity, and State Foreign Policy Interests", in *The Limits of Culture: Islam and Foreign Policy,* Brenda Shaffer (ed.), Cambridge: MIT Press, 2006; Roman Muzalevsky, "The US and Azerbaijan: Unraveling a Strategic Partnership?", *Eurasia Daily Monitor,* 7 (87), 2010; Nargiz Mehdiyeva, *Power Games in the Caucasus: Azerbaijan's Foreign and Energy Policy Towards the West, Russia and the Middle East.* London: I.B.Tauris & Co Ltd, 2011; Pinar Ipek, "Azerbaijan's Foreign Policy and Challenges for Energy Security", *Middle East Journal,* 63(2), 2009: 227-239.
107 Anar Valiyev, "Azerbaijan-Russian Relations After Five Day War: Friendship, Enmity or Pragmatism", Turkish Policy Quarterly 10 (3), 2011: 133-143.
108 Farid Ismayilzade, "Azerbaijan's Tough Foreign Policy Choices", UNISCI Discussion Papers, October, 2004.
109 Mehdiyeva, *Power Games in the Caucasus.*
110 Kamal Makili-Aliyev, "Azerbaijan's Foreign Policy: Between East and West", *IAI Working Papers,* 13 (5), 2013.
111 David Flemes and Steven Lobell, "Contested Leadership in International Relations", *International Politics,* 52 (2), 2015: 139-146.

weaker states to avoid making an obvious choice that lie between the two extremes balancing and bandwagoning."[112]

In this regard, I employ "soft balancing" to explain Azerbaijan's foreign policy behaviour. The article posits that Azerbaijan's behaviour has changed according to the shift in the level of external threat, and that factors that have affected the level of threat posed by Russia are aggregate power and offensive capabilities, proximity, and aggressive intentions. The next pages will discuss these factors where appropriate. Nonetheless, it is worthwhile to consider that the power asymmetry and geographic vicinity have remained unchanged for more than two decades, thus having the same effect on Azerbaijan's foreign policy. What has changed, though, is Azerbaijani leaders' perceptions of Russia's intentions towards the country and the region in general.

Bandwagoning under the Mutalibov Government

In the wake of the failed coup attempt against Russian President Mikhail Gorbachev in August 1991, pro-independence demonstrations in Azerbaijan intensified and resulted in the Supreme Soviet of Azerbaijan adopting a resolution on 31 August 1991 that called for independence from the USSR. This was followed by a presidential election on 8 September 1991, which was boycotted by the opposition, leaving the last leader of the Communist Party of the Azerbaijan SSR, Ayaz Mutalibov, as the unchallenged victor. The parliament subsequently passed a resolution declaring the independence of the Republic of Azerbaijan, with Mutalibov as its first president.

Mutalibov was a supporter of Gorbachev's New Union Treaty plans, that envisaged giving more autonomy to the constituent republics while preserving the Soviet Union. As such, in his address to parliament, Mutalibov argued that if Azerbaijan chose to be part of the New Union Treaty, Moscow would not be able to dictate the policies of the country like it had previously. Instead, Moscow would only direct foreign and security policy, which would be coordinated with Baku.[113] However, in newly independent Azerbaijan, anti-Russian sentiment was strong, especially in light of escalating losses in the Karabakh conflict with Armenia.

---

112 Flemes and Lobell, "Contested Leadership in International Relations", 143.
113 Elkhan Mekhtiev, "Security Policy in Azerbaijan", *NATO-EAPC Research Fellowship Project*, 2001, accessed 27.08.2018, http://www.nato.int/acad/fellow/99-01/mekhtiev.pdf.

Therefore, Mutalibov's kowtowing to Moscow provoked fierce domestic opposition. Yet regardless of the heightened concerns at home, and despite the parliament's unanimous vote against it, in December 1991, Mutalibov signed the declaration forming the CIS.

Aware of Russia's economic and military potential, Mutalibov believed refusing to sign would have left Azerbaijan politically and economically isolated, thus creating a serious problem for the country's security. According to Mutalibov himself, the President of the Russian Federation, Boris Yeltsin, offered to dismantle the 366th Motorised Infantry Brigade of the Russian Interior Ministry forces (which later took part in the massacre in the town of Khojaly), in exchange for the Azerbaijani parliament's ratification of the country's CIS membership.[114] Mutalibov also sought to join the CSTO which, in his strategic assessment, would have created better chances for Azerbaijan to preserve its control over Nagorno-Karabakh.[115]

Mutalibov was widely seen as "Moscow's man," so it is not surprising that he had a pro-Russian political orientation, which was so strong that he viewed his country's relations with other regional powers, such as Turkey and Iran, through the prism of Moscow.[116] His strategy of dealing with Russia can best be understood as a strategy of bandwagoning that was both defensive and offensive. It was defensive because he believed that by staying loyal to Russia, he would neutralise Moscow in the Karabakh conflict. It was also offensive, because Mutalibov wanted to profit from Russia by aligning with Moscow against Yerevan. In other words, his strategy was largely driven by his view of Russia as a force whose support was essential to prevent military action by Armenia against Azerbaijan.

Yet, Yerevan's offensive into Azerbaijani territories continued, and reached its climax when Armenian military formations massacred civilians in Khojaly in February 1992.[117] In the aftermath, Mutalibov was forced to resign. After his departure, Yagub Mamedov, the speaker of the parliament, became acting president until the presidential elections

---

114 Shamkhal Abilov and Ismayil Isayev, "Azerbaijan-Russia Relations: Azerbaijan's Pursuit of Successful Balanced Foreign Policy", *OAKA*, 9 (19), 2015, 113-143.

115 Mehdiyeva, *Power Games in the Caucasus*, 84.

116 James C. MacDougall, "Post-Soviet Strategic Alignment: the Weight of History in the South Caucasus", PhD diss., Washington: Georgetown University, 2009, 222-227.

117 On February 25 and 26, 1992, more than 600 civilians were killed, and several hundred more went missing. Autopsies by the International Committee for the Red Cross indicated that numerous dead bodies were mutilated.

on 8 June 1992, which were won by Abulfaz Elchibey, the chairman of the Popular Front of Azerbaijan (PFA), with just over fifty-five percent of the vote.

Hard Balancing Attempts during the Elchibey Presidency

After Abulfaz Elchibey (né Aliyev) assumed the role of President of Azerbaijan, his nascent PFA government pursued a proactive foreign policy that is usually described as anti-Russian.[118] While this is a generally accepted characterisation of his foreign policy, what is often disregarded is that Elchibey did try to establish mutually beneficial relations with Russia at the beginning of his tenure. For instance, he made his first official visit as the President of Azerbaijan to Moscow in October 1992, where, with his Russian counterpart, he signed the Treaty on Friendship, Cooperation and Mutual Security. As argued by Elkhan Mekthiyev, the fact that Elchibey chose Russia as the destination for his first official visit indicates the PFA government's recognition of Russia's important role in the region and "Azerbaijan's willingness to develop friendly and equal relations with it."[119] Nonetheless, relations started to worsen from early January 1993.

Some local scholars have pointed to several key reasons for the decline in bilateral relations between Baku and Moscow under the PFA government. First, Russia was becoming increasingly dissatisfied with the growing Western presence in the region. Moscow's concern was intensified as President Elchibey prepared to sign a deal with Western energy companies for the use of Azerbaijani oil fields, while Russian companies were left out. Secondly, Elchibey's policies aimed at refusing Russia's plans to re-establish its sphere of influence through the CIS and the continuation its military bases in the country. President Elchibey initiated the creation of Azerbaijan's new currency (the manat) and was poised to remove the country from the ruble zone.[120] He also refused to join the CIS—an organisation, according to him, that served the Russian purpose of

---

118 Shirin Hunter, *Transcaucasus in Transition: Nation Building and Conflict*, Washington, DC: The Center For Strategic and International Studies, 1996; Shirin Hunter, "Azerbaijan: Searching for new Neighbours," in I. Bremmer and R. Taras (eds.), *New States, New Politics: Building the Post-Soviet Nations*, Cambridge: Cambridge University Press, 1997.
119 Elkhan Mekhtiev, "Security Policy in Azerbaijan", 17.
120 Audrey L. Altstadt, "Azerbaijan and Aliyev: A Long History and an Uncertain Future", *Problems of Post-Communism*, 50 (5), 2003: 3-13.

keeping "the old empire in a new form" through various new mechanisms.[121] In addition, Elchibey rejected the OSCE proposal to deploy Russian observers to the Lachin region on the Armenia–Azerbaijan border; this was received with antagonism in Moscow.

One should note that Elchibey's efforts to distance Azerbaijan from Russia were taking place in the midst of Armenia's growing military intervention in Azerbaijani territories. Elchibey and other PFA leaders saw Russia as a primary supporter of these actions, leading them to openly prioritise the establishment of close relations with the West and Turkey, while disengaging from Moscow. Elchibey considered close relations with Turkey to be particularly important for Azerbaijan, because, in his own words, the country represented the "most important bridge to the world, both because Turkey is a modern state and because it is a European and an Asian country at one and the same time."[122] Thus, as a secular and democratic state with a Muslim society, Turkey was seen by Elchibey as a model for Azerbaijan to follow in order to integrate with the West. The president's foreign policy involved an attempt to pass the buck of the Russian threat to the West. The main driving force behind this endeavour was a desire "to reduce or hamper aggressive Russian policies and distance it from Azerbaijan."[123] He seemed to believe that the Russian elite was driven by neo-imperial ambitions that needed to be confronted. Elchibey's strategic assessment is likely to have been influenced by the fact that Russia's geographical proximity and its preponderance would have made it fairly easy for Moscow to reoccupy Azerbaijan. Therefore, in order to prevent this, Baku had to establish relations as close as possible with the West and Turkey.

Generally, when a leader employs a strategy, they make a cost-benefit calculation: but Elchibey's calculation appeared to be wrong, with his government's attempts to hard balance against Russia triggering an aggressive reaction from Moscow. Threatened by Azerbaijan's pro-Western and pro-Turkish foreign policy orientation, Russia encouraged the ethnic Lezghi community in the north of the country to make secessionist demands. Moscow also increased its economic, political, and military support for Armenia. In the meantime, the situation in the Nagorno-Karabakh conflict was deteriorating. A major blow came in 1993 when strategically crucial Kelbajar—a district of Azerbaijan outside

---

121 Interview with Abulfaz Elchibey, *Literaturnaya Gazeta*, 4 March 1998.
122 Ibid.
123 Interview with Abulfaz Elchibey, ANS TV. 26 November 1998.

of the administrative boundaries of Nagorno-Karabakh—was invaded. In the aftermath, to make matters worse, the former military commander, Surat Huseynov, started an open military rebellion against President Elchibey. Fearing a civil war in the country, Elchibey was forced to ask the Soviet-era leader of Azerbaijan, Heydar Aliyev, for help to resolve the internal crisis, while he himself left the capital on 24 June 1993.

Elchibey clearly believed that Moscow was an immediate threat to Azerbaijan's very survival and that Russian military action against Baku was a real possibility. From his perspective, the only option for Baku to protect itself was through integration with Western institutions. However, his overt opposition to Russia focused Moscow's enmity and eventually cost him the presidency. Furthermore, he tried to ally the country with Turkey, which was not ready to fashion an alliance against Russia.

In August 1993, a nationwide referendum in Azerbaijan resulted in a vote of no confidence in the self-exiled Elchibey. In October, new presidential elections took place that resulted in victory for Heydar Aliyev, who subsequently appointed Surat Huseynov as prime minister, in order to avoid a confrontation.

Soft Balancing under the Heydar and Ilham Aliyev Governments

Heydar Aliyev assumed the office in the midst of economic, political, and security crises. Domestically, he had to take measures to deal with problems including ethnic tensions among Lezgin and Talysh communities, as well as an economic crisis that was the result of long-term instability. In foreign policy, the primary task remained the same: to preserve Azerbaijan's independence and to restore its territorial integrity. Reinforcing independence required taking actions that would reduce and undermine Russian and Iranian attempts to influence Azerbaijan's domestic and foreign affairs. Having witnessed the results of Elchibey's overt stance against Russia and Iran, Aliyev understood that he needed to adopt a careful and delicate strategy that would neither sacrifice Azerbaijani interests nor antagonise its powerful neighbours.

President Aliyev shared with his predecessor the view that Russia aspired for regional hegemony by influencing Azerbaijan, and thus represented a challenge to the country's sovereignty and independence. However, he appeared not to view Russia as an immediate threat and understood that any attempt to form a military alliance against Moscow would only generate more aggression against Baku. As observed by Shale Horowitz and Michal Tyburski, Aliyev recognised that "defying Russia in any significant way would lead Russia to support internal opposition elements that might overthrow his rule."[124] Hence, Azerbaijan under his leadership adopted a pragmatic and non-ideological foreign policy doctrine that is often referred to, even by Azerbaijani officials, as the "balanced foreign policy."

According to the current Azerbaijani minister of foreign affairs, Elmar Mammadyarov, the aim of the "balanced foreign policy" that Azerbaijan has pursued since 1993 is to find "a *modus vivendi* with regional and non-regional actors which pursue their own, sometimes divergent, policies."[125] Similarly, Jason Strakes describes "balanced foreign policy" as an "informal realist approach," that has sought "to preserve the country's autonomy while deriving beneficial resources from constructive engagements with three major geopolitical actors (United States, Russia, and Iran), despite their attendant liabilities for Azerbaijani national interests."[126] Indeed, the "balanced foreign policy" is effectively a realist approach to foreign policy, mainly because it is driven by motivations of self-interest and to ensure self-preservation. As a doctrine, it identifies the guiding principles and strategic vision for Azerbaijani foreign policy. In line with the "balanced foreign policy," distinct and even mixed foreign policy strategies can be employed that may involve low concessions towards powerful actors, without compromising the country's national interests whenever they clash with those of major states. As explained by Heydar Aliyev: "You cannot be friends with some countries and enemies with others despite the fact that this is the way most countries function. Azerbaijan does not want to be an enemy with any country. At the same time, we will not become victim to another country's policies. Azerbaijan has its own independent policy."[127] In this chapter, I argue that as part

---

124 Shale Horowitz and Michael D. Tyburski, "Reacting to Russia: Foreign Relations of the Former Soviet Bloc", in *Beyond Great Powers And Hegemons: Why Secondary States Support, Follow Or Challenge*, Kristen P. Williams, Steven E. Lobell, and Neal G. Jesse (eds.), California : Stanford University Press, 2012, 168.

125 Elmar Mammadyarov, "The Foreign Policy of Azerbaijan: Affecting Factor and Strategic Priorities", in *Azerbaijan in Global Politics: Crafting Foreign Policy*, Alexandros Petersen and Fariz Ismailzade (eds.). Baku: Azerbaijan Diplomatic Academy, 2009, 20.

126 Jason E. Strakes, "Situating the 'Balanced Foreign Policy': The Role of System Structure in Azerbaijan's Multi-Vector diplomacy", *Journal of Balkan and Near Eastern Studies*, 15 (1), 2013: 38.

127 Quoted in Strakes, "Azerbaijan and the Non-Aligned Movement: Institutionalising the Balanced Foreign Policy Doctrine", *IAI Working Papers,* 15 (11), 2015: 2.

of the "balanced foreign policy", President Aliyev employed a strategy of soft balancing that is the most appropriate concept to explain how Azerbaijan has pursued its foreign policy objectives.

In relations with Russia, soft balancing was employed to offset and undermine the country's attempts to influence the domestic and foreign affairs of Azerbaijan, while also engaging with Moscow. Thus, this strategy comprised patterns of balancing, which took a non-military and more indirect shape. In this respect, Baku has largely protected its real strategic intentions and has balanced against Russia through less provocative means. Yet, Baku also pursued cooperative relations with Moscow in some areas.

As part of his strategy, President Aliyev made a number of decisions that are usually seen as accommodating Moscow's interests. For instance, shortly after he came to power, Aliyev announced that the country would join the CIS. However, he was certainly not interested in consolidating the organisation. According to Thomas Goltz, Aliyev merely paid "lip service" to Moscow, without "implementing any of the agreements in a meaningful way."[128] In fact, membership of the CIS could have constituted "institutional balancing," which is a form of soft balancing. Kai He argues that states pursue institutional balancing through multilateral institutions. According to him, there are two forms of institutional balancing: inclusive and exclusive balancing. "While the former refers to binding the target states in the institution, the lateral means keeping the target states out. In inclusive institutional balancing, states practice norm/rule-building to constrain other states' behaviour or control and manipulate agendas to address issues related to their interests in multilateral institutions. In exclusive balancing, states consolidate their political and economic unity to resist pressures from outsiders."[129] For this reason, Aliyev's decision to enter the CIS could have stemmed from the desire to constrain Moscow's behaviour through institutional balancing.

The strained relations with Russia did not immediately improve, even after Azerbaijan joined the CIS. In fact, the bilateral relationship continued to worsen during the First Chechen War (1994–1996). Moscow accused Azerbaijan of giving shelter to Chechen fighters—claims that were rejected by Baku. As a result, Russia closed its borders with Azerbaijan in 1994 and imposed an economic embargo for three years. Russian

---

128 Thomas Goltz, *Azerbaijani Diary: A Rogue Reporter's Adventures in an Oil-Rich, War-Torn, Post-Soviet Republic*, New York: Sharpe, 1999, 446.
129 He, "Institutional Balancing", 493.

allegations have never been proved. As Audrey Altstadt has pointed out, in the face of the secessionist threat from the Karabakh Armenians, supporting a secessionist movement in Russia was something that Azerbaijan could not afford.[130] However, for the sake of theoretical discussion, even if Russian allegations were to be true, this would only mean that Azerbaijan was engaging in a soft balancing act, because, as discussed earlier, one of the mechanisms for soft balancing is to provide aid to rivals of the threatening power.

Aliyev's first major soft balancing act did not take place until the country initiated energy projects. From the early years of his regime, Heydar Aliyev paid significant attention to natural resources as the potential driver to overcome the economic crisis, but also as the most important tool to pursue the country's foreign policy goals. Therefore, as soon as he came to power, Aliyev launched fresh talks with oil companies. However, his efforts to reach a deal for the development of the Azeri–Chiraq–Gunashli (ACG) fields in the Caspian Sea met with opposition from some segments inside the Russian elite, who believed that the newly independent littoral states had no sovereignty over their zones of the Caspian Sea and thus made great efforts to obstruct it. Aliyev managed to overcome this opposition by granting a share in the Azerbaijan International Operating Company (AIOC), a consortium of foreign companies, to the Russian oil company, Lukoil. Thereafter, despite the challenges, the "contract of the century" was signed on 20 September 1994.

The participation of Lukoil in the AIOC consortium led to Moscow's de facto recognition of Azerbaijan's right to exercise its sovereignty over its sector of the Caspian Sea. In the words of Terry Adams, first president of the AIOC: "Heydar Aliyev was clear in his choice of investors. They had to include major oil companies with an international track record and reputation for successful project delivery ... But the president primarily saw such a broad range of foreign investors with a diversity of national interests as being the mechanism from which he could build Azeri foreign policy, and secure national stability."[131]

Having neutralised Russia's claims against Azerbaijan's sovereign rights over its energy resources, Aliyev focused on transportation routes. It was a particularly challenging issue, because Moscow—following the demise of the Soviet Union—has sought to use the Soviet-era

---

130 Altstadt, "Azerbaijan and Aliyev", 12.
131 Quoted in Mehdiyeva, *Power Games in the Caucasus*, 136.

transportation network to monopolise oil and gas exports to Europe, in order to exert influence on the post-Soviet countries and to gain political leverage vis-à-vis the West. Aware of the dangers of relying solely on Russia for the transportation of oil, Azerbaijan and international oil companies wanted to ensure the flow of energy to Europe free from Russian control.[132] However, ignoring and isolating Moscow could have provoked an aggressive Russian reaction. Therefore, the Baku–Novorossiysk Pipeline, the 1,400-km-long route connecting the Caspian Sea to the Black Sea through Russia, was selected and approved as one of the two "early oil" routes, which became operational in 1997.

By allowing the low-capacity pipeline through Russia to function, Baku, on the one hand, found a solution to its dispute with Russia over the Caspian seabed, and, on the other, ensured the flow of energy in case of possible instability in Georgia.

While one of the first routes for "early oil" was through Russia, it was decided that the main export pipeline would go through Tbilisi to the Turkish port of Ceyhan on the Mediterranean. The Baku–Tbilisi–Ceyhan (BTC) Oil Pipeline, more than 1,700 kilometres long, became operational in 2006. Thanks to this project, Baku has grown economically self-sufficient, but has also further strengthened its independence, sovereignty, and political autonomy. As has been rightly pointed out, "multibillion oil revenues that boosted the country's economy and strengthened its internal capacity also worked to lift its self-confidence, including in its relations with Russia and the West."[133] The realisation of the BTC Pipeline was the outcome of a strategic decision that reflects Baku's exercise of soft balancing vis-á-vis Russia.

Aliyev utilised Azerbaijan's energy potential to secure economic independence from Russia as well as support for that independence from Western countries. In the opinion of Brenda Shaffer, the choice of the Turkish–Georgian route indicates "the view that a security alliance with these states brought it [Azerbaijan] the most benefit among its various regional options and was the least risky to have dependence on these states versus others."[134] A similar conclusion was reached by Meister, who argued

132 Shirin Akiner, "Politics of Energy in the Caspian Region", in *Eastern Europe, Russia and Central Asia,* Dominic Heaney, ed. London: Routledge, 2011.

133 Murad Ismayilov, "Power, Knowledge, and Pipelines: Understanding the Politics of Azerbaijan's Foreign Policy", *Caucasus Survey* 2, (1–2), 2014: 92.

134 Brenda Shaffer, "Foreign Policies of the States of the Caucasus: Evolution in the Post-Soviet Period", *Uluslararası İlişkiler,* 7 (26), 2010: 58.

that "in choosing Georgia as a key partner for its independent resource exports, Baku has gained an opportunity to become more economically independent from Russia."[135] Overall, Heydar Aliyev, during the years of his presidency, managed to stabilise the country and "maintained the independence of his small state despite pressure and incursions by two powerful neighbors, Iran and Russia."[136] He also successfully "struck a balance in the country's relations with most of its neighbours and also among the major powers with interests in Azerbaijan and its oil."[137]

Azerbaijan's relations with Russia improved even further after Vladimir Putin came to power. Presidents Aliyev and Putin quickly established sympathetic personal relations and, ever since, bilateral relations have generally been characterised by friendly rhetoric. Over the years, Baku and Moscow came to an agreement on the legal status of the Caspian Sea and trade turnover has grown significantly, reaching $2.6 billion in 2017.[138] It is worth mentioning that Baku has also became one of the main importers of Russian armaments. In general, at an official level, the bilateral relationship is described as a "strategic partnership, based on the principles of equality, good-neighbourliness, centuries-old traditions of friendship, a common history and culture."[139] Nonetheless, some of Russia's actions have still at times threatened Azerbaijan's own interests, to which Baku has continued to respond through soft balancing. The establishment of the Organization for Democracy and Economic Development (GUAM) as a regional institution that has strategically isolated Russia, is a good example of exclusive institutional balancing that has been initiated under Heydar Aliyev and later continued by his son Ilham Aliyev, who became President of Azerbaijan in 2003.

Although one of the first foreign policy decisions after the Heydar Aliyev government came to power was to join the CIS, Azerbaijan seemed to be interested in keeping the organisation as loose as possible. By the mid-1990s, it was clear that the CIS was composed of groups of countries that had diverging, if not mutually exclusive, interests, as well

---

135 Meister, "Hedging and Wedging: Strategies to Contest Russia's Leadership in Post-Soviet Eurasia", 316.
136 Altstadt, "Azerbaijan and Aliyev: A Long History and an Uncertain Future", 3.
137 Ibid., 10.
138 Azernews, "Zakharova: Russia, Azerbaijan linked By Strategic Partnership Relations", April, 2018, accessed 27.08.2018, https://www.azernews.az/nation/130794.html.
139 Ibid.

as foreign policy orientations.[140] In this regard, Azerbaijan's objectives largely coincided with those of Georgia, Moldova, and Ukraine—more "independent-minded" states that had also suffered from separatism on their territories, except for Ukraine, which at that time was merely concerned about separatist demands. Within the space of a few years, these countries have intensified their multilateral interaction, which was acknowledged in a joint communiqué between their leaders during the Council of Europe meeting in Strasbourg in October 1997. At that event, the heads of Georgia, Ukraine, Azerbaijan, and Moldova, officially launched the GUAM group. GUAM was formalised as an organisation at the Yalta Summit in 2001, when the five founding countries signed a formal charter (Uzbekistan joined the group in April 1999, at which time it became known as GUUAM, but withdrew in 2005).

Some scholars have characterised GUAM as an attempt to "balance the military and economic power and influence of Russia."[141] Similarly, Russian policymakers have viewed the organisation as directed against Russia, as can easily be seen from the statement of then Foreign Minister of Russian Federation, Igor Ivanov: "We should call things by their correct names: GUUAM is a political organisation with plans to transform itself into a military and political one."[142]

Yet GUAM is not an attempt to balance Russia's capabilities. In fact, the possibility of GUAM becoming an effective counterweight to Russia in terms of material balance has always been very low.[143] Therefore, GUAM members have always been careful not to portray the organisation as an alliance against Russia. That explains why member states frequently reiterate that GUAM "is not directed against third countries or a group of countries."[144] However, that is not to say that balancing motives are absent from GUAM's functions: in fact, this article argues that the main driver behind the formation of GUAM is soft balancing motives. In other words, GUAM's main purpose is to counter Russia diplomatically, politically, and economically. This conclusion was supported by Adrian Hyde-Price in two short sentences: "GUUAM has never

---

140 Taras Kuzio, "Geopolitical Pluralism in the CIS: the Emergence of GUUAM", *European Security*, 9 (2), 2000: 81-114.

141 MacDougall, *Post-Soviet Strategic Alignment*, 248-249.

142 See the interview with Igor Ivanov in *Komsomol'skaya pravda*, 20 July 1999.

143 Barry Buzan and Ole Wæver, *Regions and Powers: the Structure of International Security*, Cambridge: Cambridge University Press, 2009.

144 Ministry of Foreign Affairs of Republic of Moldova, "About GUAM", accessed 27.08.2018, http://www.mfa.gov.md/about-guam-en/.

functioned as a means of 'hard balancing' against Russian power. At best, it constitutes a form of 'soft balancing,' signalling a political intent to resist Russian hegemony and explore other foreign policy options."[145]

Another regional development that has heightened Baku's security concerns in the twenty-first century was the Russo-Georgian War in 2008, which was followed by an agreement between Moscow and Yerevan to extend Russia's lease of the 102nd military base in Gyumri until 2044. In the light of these developments, Azerbaijan during Ilham Aliyev's presidency has continued to pursue a soft balancing strategy, aimed at minimising threats to the country's economic and political stability and ensuring its survival. One of the earliest soft balancing responses was the denial of Azerbaijan's territory to Russia.

Although Azerbaijan managed to secure the departure of the Russian troops from its territory during the Elchibey presidency, Moscow continued to have one last military foothold in Azerbaijan: the Soviet-era radar station located in the northern city of Gabala. Built during the Cold War, the base was equipped with an early warning system to detect ballistic missiles between continents, and it had the capacity to determine military movements in the southern hemisphere.[146] Following the collapse of the Soviet Union, the Russian Aerospace Defence Forces continued to operate the base, even though there was no inter-state agreement. During Heydar Aliyev's visit to Moscow in January 2002, Azerbaijan and Russia signed an agreement to lease the base until December 2012. According to the agreement, in addition to $15 million for electricity and other expenses, Russia had to pay $7 million as a rental fee.

When negotiations started for a new lease agreement, Baku initially increased the fee from $7 million to $15 million per year, then, in early 2012, asked to increase the fee to $150 million and, later to $300 million per year. When asked about Azerbaijan's proposal, the spokesperson of the presidential administration, Elnur Aslanov, commented that it "reflects today's realities."[147] In a similar vein, Member of Parliament Asim Mollazade defended the proposal, by saying that Azerbaijan did

145 Adrian Hyde-Price, *European Security in the Twenty-First Century: The Challenge of Multipolarity*, London: Routledge, 2007, 147.
146 Sinan Oghan, "Gabala Radar Station: 'Somebody is Watching Us'", *TURKSAM*, January 1, 2000, accessed 27.08.2018 , https://web.archive.org/web/20120521194641/http://www.turksam .org/en/yazdir120.html.
147 Shahin Abbasov, "Azerbaijan: Signs Point to Russia's Departure from Gabala Radar Base", Eurasia.net, 25 July 2012 , accessed 27.08.2018 , https://eurasianet.org/s/azerbaijan -signs-point-to-russias-departure-from-gabala-radar-base.

not need the radar station and it would be better if the base operated as "the Dinosaur Museum of the Cold War."[148] As a result, Russia withdrew from the facility at the end of 2012.

By increasing the rental fee from $7 million to $300 million, Azerbaijan simply signalled that Baku did not want the Russian base, as a strategic response to the 2008 war and Russia's decision to maintain its military base in Armenia. In doing so, Azerbaijani policymakers carried out a soft balancing act in a manner that made it difficult for Russia to retaliate, especially by emphasising the non-political nature of Azerbaijan's decision, but also, reportedly, by Baku convincing Moscow that the facility would not be leased to any other state. In this regard, when asked about Russia's departure, former Head of the External Relations Department in Azerbaijan's Presidential Administration, Novruz Mammadov, argued that the closure was financial and not political in nature.[149]

Under the Ilham Aliyev government, Azerbaijan also continued to engage in soft balancing through economic strengthening, by initiating and implementing new energy and transportation projects. Azerbaijan launched and is currently implementing the Southern Gas Corridor (SGC) that will consist of several pipelines. Once the project is finalised, European countries will be supplied with natural gas from Azerbaijan's fields in the Caspian Sea. The strategic importance of the SGC stems from the fact that it runs from Azerbaijan through Georgia and Turkey to reach Greece and Italy while bypassing Russian territory, thus improving the EU's energy security by reducing the import dependency on Moscow.

In the initial phase, it is planned that six billion cubic metres (bcm) of natural gas per year will be transported to Europe. The volumes are expected to increase to ten bcm from 2020. But, the SGC is being built with capacity for transporting up to thirty-one bcm of natural gas annually to the European market, which means other gas producing countries may join the project in the future.[150]

In recent years, Azerbaijan has also actively worked to revive the transportation projects that are alternatives to the Russian route. To this

---

148 Ibid.
149 Anar Valiyev, "Russia to Cease Using Gabala Radar Station", the Jamestown Foundation Commentaries, December 14, 2012, accessed 27.08.2018, https://jamestown.org/russia-to-cease-using-gabala-radar-station/.
150 Fuad Shahbazov, "Southern Gas Corridor Project Opening New Long-Term Opportunities for Europe", *Eurasia Daily Monitor*, 15 (88), 2018, accessed 27.08.2018, https://jamestown.org/program/southern-gas-corridor-project-opening-new-long-term-opportunities-for-europe/.

direction, Azerbaijan along with Georgia and Turkey launched the 826-km Baku–Tbilisi–Kars (BTK) railway. This extends from the Azerbaijani shores of the Caspian Sea, through Georgia, to the east of Turkey, from where it links up to the Turkish railway system that is directly connected to Europe. The project complements the southern dimension of the new Silk Road network between China and Europe.[151]

Since it became operational in 2017, goods can be transported from China to Europe via the BTK in 15 days, bypassing Russia. Hence, the successful realisation of the railway enables Azerbaijan, Georgia, and Turkey together to emerge as one of the major transport corridors between Europe and East Asia. As a result, Samuel Lussac notes that Russia may feel threatened that the BTK will undermine Moscow's influence in the region.[152]

As Elias Götz has observed, hegemony-seeking states generally seek "to secure lines of communication and trade routes in their vicinity and maintain access to strategically important locations near their border."[153] In this respect, Azerbaijani-initiated energy and transportation projects have served several strategic purposes. First, their successful implementation has enabled Azerbaijan to diversify its trade relations, thus decreasing its economic dependency on Russia. They have also served to undermine Russia's economic power and help to reduce Moscow's grip on the Caspian Basin energy exports.

Conclusion

Since Azerbaijan regained its independence from the Soviet Union, its core foreign and security objectives have remained unchanged: restoring the country's territorial integrity and preserving its independence, which requires ensuring complete sovereignty over foreign and domestic matters, securing its economic self-sufficiency, and guaranteeing the security of the Azerbaijani people from real and potential external

---

151 Wade Shepard, Reconnecting Asia: The Story Behind The Emerging Baku-Tbilisi-Kars Rail Line, Forbes, December 15, 2016, accessed 04.03.2019, https://www.forbes.com/sites/wadeshepard/2016/12/15/reconnecting-asia-the-story-behind-the-emerging-baku-tbilisi-kars-rail-line/#3afb86753978.

152 Samuel Lussac, "The Baku-Tbilisi-Kars Railroad and Its Geopolitical Implications for the South Caucasus", *Caucasus Review of International Affairs* 2 (4), 2008.

153 Elias Götz, Neorealism and Russia's Ukraine policy, 1991–present, Contemporary Politics 22 (3), 2016, 301-323.

threats. In this respect, Russia's political agenda in the region and its actions have been a major concern for Azerbaijani leaders, albeit while not constituting an immediate threat to Azerbaijan's survival as an independent republic. Nevertheless, throughout the 1990s, Russian governments, with the aim of keeping Azerbaijan within their orbit, used various tools to destabilise the country: triggering ethnic separatism, civil unrest, and provoking economic crisis, as confirmed by some Azerbaijani officials. Russia also overtly or covertly has established the geopolitical and geoeconomic blockade around Azerbaijan, supporting Armenia's military occupation, while pressuring Azerbaijanis living in Russia and taking other measures to intentionally damage the national interests of Azerbaijan.[154]

Although after Vladimir Putin came to power in 2000, Russian foreign policy took a more pragmatic character, leading to some improvement in bilateral relations, Moscow continues to see itself as the regional hegemon with special rights and obligations. In the face of hegemony-seeking Russia, Azerbaijani governments have opted for different strategies. This chapter's main aim has been to explain how and why Azerbaijan has reacted to Russia's threatening policies.

The history of Azerbaijani–Russian relations between 1991 and 2017 reveals that, except for a short period under President Mutalibov (1991–1992), Baku has refrained from aligning itself with Moscow. Similarly, for a brief period in 1992–1993, Azerbaijan tried to pursue external balancing by establishing closer relations with the West and NATO member Turkey. This strategy of hard balancing was largely the result of the perception of President Elchibey of the aggressive intentions of Russia, and it proved to be highly costly and less effective as it focused the enmity on Russia, which retaliated even more aggressively against Baku. Since 1993, Azerbaijan has maintained a foreign policy strategy that can be best characterised as soft balancing. This strategy was first employed by Heydar Aliyev immediately after he came to power in 1993. Ilham Aliyev, who succeeded Heydar Aliyev in 2003, continues to deploy soft balancing, with more emphasis on economic statecraft.

The chapter discussed in detail the dynamics of Azerbaijan's oil diplomacy and pipeline politics, as a strategy of economic strengthening and achieving economic independence from Russia. It came to the conclusion that the real strategic motivation behind Aliyev's politicking

---

154 Hasanov, *Azerbaydzhanin Geosiyaseti*, 245.

was to soft balance Moscow. Developing the economic capabilities of Azerbaijan has not only enabled Baku to strengthen its relations with other former Soviet republics and Western countries, but also extended its external ties with African, Asian, and Latin American countries, thus making it difficult for Moscow to upset Azerbaijan's foreign relations.

Similarly, the chapter analysed the processes behind the formation of GUAM, which served the purpose of reinforcing national independence and increasing cooperation with the West. By taking an active role in the establishment of the GUAM group, Baku has signalled the possibility of participating in a balancing coalition against Russia by cooperating with the West. However, Baku has been careful not to establish any formal alliance, which would risk an immediate reaction from Moscow.

When it comes to its effectiveness, it must be said that Azerbaijan's use of soft balancing has not completely eradicated security threats against the country. In fact, Russia continues to be Armenia's main security ally and still carries out policies that undermine some of Azerbaijan's interests. Nevertheless, by engaging in soft balancing, Azerbaijan has been able to offset and minimise the scale of threats to Baku's stability and survival, without risking a confrontation with Moscow.

As a distinct strategy, in line with Azerbaijan's "balanced foreign policy" doctrine, soft balancing contains mixed patterns of balancing that have taken non-military and more indirect shape and cooperation in a number of areas. While engaging in balancing against Russia, Baku has protected its real strategic intentions and has used less provocative means, thus reducing the risk of Russia's otherwise aggressive retaliation. In other words, to borrow the term offered by Medeiros Evan, Azerbaijan's soft balancing has been a "geopolitical insurance strategy."[155]

---

155 Evan S. Medeiros, "Strategic Hedging and the Future of Asia Pacific Stability", *The Washington Quarterly*, 29 (1), 2005: 145-167.

CHAPTER 3
Azerbaijani-EU Relations: More Opportunities on the Horizon

Anar Valiyev

Introduction

The history of relations between Azerbaijan and the European Union dates back to 1999, when both sides worked together to sign a number of important political documents, including the EU–Azerbaijan Partnership and Cooperation Agreement. That agreement envisioned strengthening cooperation in trade, investment, economy, legislation, and culture.[156] By 2009, the country joined the EU-led European Neighborhood Policy (ENP) and became a member of the Eastern Partnership Initiative. Both sides subsequently worked closely in trying to solve a number of issues, ranging from trade to visa facilitation. However, in 2017—when Ukraine, Moldova, and Georgia all signed Association Agreements and established visa-free regimes—Azerbaijan instead decided to distance itself from EU integration.[157]

Baku and Brussels look at each other with hope, and understand the immense potential of cooperation. However, several issues have complicated the relationship. For the EU, Azerbaijan's strategic location and Europe's dependency on external supplies of gas and oil make it a valuable partner. For its part, Azerbaijan looks to the EU as a market for

---

156 European Commission, "EU-Azerbaijan Partnership and Cooperation Agreement", 1999, accessed 08.08.2018, https://eeas.europa.eu/delegations/azerbaijan/10813/eu-azerbaijan-partnership -and-cooperation-agreement-1999_en.

157 Carmen Valache, "EU-Azerbaijan Ties Deteriorate but How Far Will Baku Drift Toward Russia?", *Intellinews*, 16 September 2015, accessed 19.01.2018, http://www.intellinews.com/eu -azerbaijanties-deteriorate-but-how-far-will-baku-drift-toward-russia-500447241/?archive=bne.

its resources and hopes that the EU can provide a counterbalance to Russia and Iran in the region, as well as assist in the resolution of the Nagorno-Karabakh conflict. However, the EU has not taken a decisive position on Nagorno-Karabakh as it has done in the cases of Crimea, Abkhazia, and South Ossetia. The differing response between this and other post-Soviet conflicts can only be explained as a "double standard." Nevertheless, EU assistance has been critical to Azerbaijan in the past; since 1991, the EU has provided more than €500 million to Azerbaijan in technical, humanitarian, emergency, and food assistance.[158]

For Azerbaijan, there are many benefits to deeper cooperation with the EU. EU investments in non-oil sectors may also be critical to Azerbaijan's efforts to diversify its economy. The government continues to negotiate a large-scale partnership agreement with the EU that envisions various areas of cooperation, including trade and political partnership.[159] For the last two years, both sides have been involved in intense discussions to agree a document on cooperation that will satisfy both sides. On 20 December 2017, Federica Mogherini, High Representative of the European Union for Foreign Affairs and Security Policy, and Vice-President of the European Commission, stated that the EU and Azerbaijan are making good progress in negotiating a new agreement. "Since the European Union and Azerbaijan signed our last bilateral agreement—the Partnership and Cooperation Agreement—in 1996, a lot has changed," she said. Mogherini stressed that together the sides "will look for more opportunities for young people to meet and to travel, possibilities for businesses to grow, to protect human rights and to facilitate energy relations, bringing real benefits to our respective citizens."[160] Both sides, meanwhile, hope that a comprehensive agreement will be signed in 2019 or 2020, heralding a new era in relations between Azerbaijan and European Union. The following chapter discusses the priorities and agenda for Azerbaijan towards integration with the European Union. It tries to explain the reasoning behind Baku's strategy of cooperating

---

158 Valiyev, Anar (2014). "Azerbaijan's Elite between Scylla and Charybdis: EU OR CUSTOMS UNION?" PONARS Eurasia Policy Memo No. 309. Accessed October 2, 2019 http://www .ponarseurasia.org/sites/default/files/policy-memos-pdf/Pepm_309_Valiyev_Feb2014.pdf.

159 Ilgar Gurbanov, "Strategic Partnership Agreement: A New Chapter in EU-Azerbaijan Relations", Eurasia Daily Monitor, Vol. 14, No. 84, 2017, accessed 27.01.2018, https://jamestown.org /program/strategic-partnership-agreement-new-chapter-eu-azerbaijan-relations.

160 APA, "EU, Azerbaijan Making Good Progress in Negotiations for New Agreement, Mogherini Says", 20 December 2017, accessed 21.05.2018, http://en.apa.az/azerbaijan-politics/foreign-news /eu-azerbaijan-making-good-progress-in-negotiations-for-new-agreement-mogherini-says .html.

with Brussels. Moreover, the chapter looks at the Azerbaijani government's attempts to build a European identity and considers whether this policy has been successful. [161]

Political Cooperation

From the EU perspective, the main objective of cooperation between Brussels and Baku is to establish an increasingly close relationship that can extend to deeper economic and political cooperation. The ENP offered a major opportunity for integration. The EU's main priorities for Azerbaijan include democratic development and good governance; socio-economic reform (with an emphasis on regulatory approximation with the EU); combatting poverty and building administrative capacity; and supporting legislative and economic reforms in the transport, energy, and environmental sectors.[162] Following the unexpected results of the EU membership referendum in the UK ("Brexit"), Baku today fears that growing scepticism in EU countries towards cooperation with non-EU members such as Belarus, Georgia, Moldova, and Ukraine will endanger future cooperation. It is reasonable to expect the EU to concentrate more on its own problems than to expand its influence into the Eastern Partnership countries. This is especially alarming for Baku, considering the recent improvement in relations with Brussels on many issues. Moreover, the Eastern Partnership countries, Azerbaijan in particular, have expressed scepticism towards EU institutions and their inability to cope with the Union's internal problems.

Analysing eight years of the Eastern Partnership Initiative and its impact on Azerbaijan raises some points of controversy. Azerbaijan was able to secure EU support for the Trans Anatolian Natural Gas Pipeline (TANAP) and Trans Adriatic Pipeline (TAP), which will transport Azerbaijani gas to Europe. Baku was also successful in negotiating visa facilitation and readmission agreements, making it easier for Azerbaijani

---

161 Anar Valiyev, "First European Olympic Games in Baku: New Articulation of Azerbaijani Identity?", in Andrey Makarychev and Alexandra Yatsyk (eds.), *2016: Mega Events in Post–Soviet Eurasia: Shifting Borderlines of Inclusion and Exclusion*, New York: Palgrave Macmillan, 2016, 131-149.

162 European Council, "Remarks by President Donald Tusk after his Meeting with President of Azerbaijan Ilham Aliyev", Press Release 47/17, 6 February 2017, accessed 21.05.2018, http://www.consilium.europa.eu/en/press/press-releases/2017/02/06-tusk-remarks-president-azerbaijan-aliyev/.

citizens to acquire a Schengen visa. These were the only successes of the programme, however. At the 2013 Vilnius Summit, it became clear that Baku is not interested in signing an Association Agreement; rather, it prefers to sign a separate Strategic Modernisation Partnership Agreement. There are several reasons for this. Russian pressure applied on Armenia and Moscow's intervention in Ukraine amidst the signing of the agreement sent alarming signals across the ENP countries, and Baku sees no significant benefit in signing such an agreement while negative factors could overshadow any success.[163] Meanwhile, the unexpected results of the Brexit referendum in the summer of 2016 significantly impacted Azerbaijanis' perceptions of European identity and their country's future cooperation with the EU. Britain has been a major investor in Azerbaijan and has played the role of Baku's EU champion. Within the EU, London has been the preeminent defender of Azerbaijani initiatives, advocating for the Baku–Tblisi–Ceyhan Gas Pipeline to Turkey and Europe, as well as several other large projects. Britain's energy interests in Azerbaijan have allowed Baku, in turn, to better promote its own interests to EU members and obtain pro-Azerbaijani resolutions or statements from the EU on the Nagorno-Karabakh (NK) issue. Although Britain's decision to leave the EU does not mean that Baku will stop cooperating with Brussels, London's absence as a major player and supporter will make it difficult for Azerbaijan to receive the same level of EU support on a range of projects. The UK has consequential influence in Azerbaijan and in the South Caucasus in general. Besides the spread of the English language, the British education system is a major destination for Azerbaijani students. About 570 Azerbaijani students have been educated or are currently studying at British universities through government-sponsored programmes, and many more (hundreds) study there through other means. It is hard to anticipate how Brexit may impact this, but the expectation is that it would be more difficult for Azerbaijani students to study in the UK because they often have come through programmes involving consortia of European universities (such as Erasmus). Brexit would halt such cooperation, and it would be difficult to secure funding from the EU for any joint projects involving British universities.[164]

---

163 Anar Valiyev, "10 Years of Eastern Partnership in Azerbaijan: Still a Long Way to Go", *Heinrich Boll Stiftung*, 13 September 2019. Retrieved 3 October 2019 https://ge.boell.org/en /2019/09/13/10-years-eastern-partnership-azerbaijan-still-long-way-go.

164 Anar Valiyev, "Brexit and Its Impact on Azerbaijan: Will East-West Integration Be Harmed?" PONARS Eurasia Policy Memo 461, 2017. http://www.ponarseurasia.org/memo

Perhaps the most important implication of Brexit on Azerbaijan is symbolic. For years, the trust of Azerbaijanis towards EU institutions was comparatively high and a majority of the population was willing to integrate into EU institutions. Brexit was the second biggest blow to trust in Azerbaijan towards the EU (the first was the Russo-Georgian War in 2008). Most people in Azerbaijan observing Brexit see the risk of disintegration of the Union, which makes them hesitant about seeking further integration with the EU. In parallel, the rise of Moscow's Eurasian Economic Union (EEU) has decreased pro-European sentiments among Azerbaijanis, both citizens and politicians.

Currently, political relations between the EU and Azerbaijan depend not only on the willingness of Baku, but also on the commitment of Brussels to engage in the region and to recognise Azerbaijan as part of Europe. Moreover, with planning for Brexit now underway, Brussels will need to increase engagement with Azerbaijan (and the region at large) on a range of issues; otherwise, further erosion of trust will occur. A positive sign is the European Council's adoption, in November 2016, of a mandate for the European Commission and the High Representative for Foreign Affairs and Security Policy to negotiate a comprehensive agreement with Azerbaijan on behalf of the EU and its member states.[165] The new agreement will replace the 1996 Partnership and Cooperation Agreement and should better address shared EU–Azerbaijani objectives and challenges. By fully engaging with Azerbaijan, the EU will be able to neutralise swiftly the regional effects of Brexit and Russian political interference. If Brussels vacillates, Azerbaijan may easily fall prey to the growing pro-Russian EEU, wiping out decades of trust-building efforts by European policymakers. Meanwhile, Russian influence has gradually increased with the weakening of EU power in the South Caucasus, especially in Azerbaijan. Russia began to re-engage with the region during the mid-2000s, aiming to attract Baku to its new model of integration. Yet Baku consistently ignored Russian initiatives: first the Customs Union, and later the EEU. Pursuing its own objective of becoming an energy hub and critical provider of European energy security, Baku saw the Russian projects as obstacles in its path to developing an independent

---

/brexit-and-its-impact-azerbaijan-will-east-west-integration-be-harmed Retrieved on 1 August 2019.

165 European Council, "EU to Launch New Negotiations on a New Agreement with Azerbaijan", 14 November 2016, accessed 14.08.2018, http://www.consilium.europa.eu/en/press/press-releases/2016/11/14/azerbaijan/.

foreign policy. In addition, the economic benefits offered by Russia were not sufficiently attractive. However, with increased Russian presence in the South Caucasus and a new wave of confrontation between Russia and the West, Baku has begun to rethink its attitude towards the EEU in the past two years—in a climate of deteriorating relations with the EU, diminished oil prices, and Russia's stance on resolving the Nagorno-Karabakh conflict. Amid all these processes, Baku needs EU political support and security guarantees comparable to those enjoyed by Ukraine or Georgia; but so far, the EU has been unable to provide either, especially in terms of a resolution to the Nagorno-Karabakh conflict.[166]

Economic Cooperation

The EU remains Azerbaijan's main economic partner. From 2011–2016, between 47% and 55% of Azerbaijan's exports went to the EU, compared to between 26% and 32% of its imports coming from the region. EU countries are also the largest investors in Azerbaijan, with the UK, Germany, and France topping the list. In 2013, total EU foreign direct investment into Azerbaijan amounted to €4.7 billion. By 2017, EU investments in Azerbaijan's fixed capital amounted to about $20 billion or 46% of the total volume of investments. Meanwhile, EU countries invested $3 billion in non-oil sectors of Azerbaijan's economy, which accounts for 35% of total investment volume in this area.[167] The EU is also a strong supporter of Azerbaijan's integration with the WTO and other organisations. However, the EU's most significant contribution to economic cooperation was, and will continue to be, the EU-sponsored transportation projects intended to connect it to East Asia, especially China. Since it gained independence, the Azerbaijani government has actively attempted to develop the country into a bridge between Europe and Asia. Since the early 1990s, the EU has initiated projects to reconnect post-Soviet states with markets in both continents. At a conference in Brussels in May 1993, the EU launched the Transport Corridor Europe–Caucasus–Asia (TRACECA) programme, as a means of spurring intermodal transport initiatives. The programme was

166 Valiyev Anar, "Azerbaijan's Foreign Policy: What Role for the West in South Caucasus", Working Paper Series, *Eastern Voices: Europe's East Faces and Unsettled West*. Washington, DC: Center for Transatlantic Relations, Johns Hopkins University, 2017.
167 Azernews, "Share of EU Countries in Azerbaijan's Turnover Increases", 8 June 2017, accessed 08.08.2018 https://www.azernews.az/business/114416.html.

revived at a summit in Baku in 1998, when TRACECA member states established the Baku-based Intergovernmental Commission and Permanent Secretariat. Since then, the EU has invested roughly $800 million in new capital projects to renovate ports, railroads, and roads along the TRACECA corridor.

Member states have also taken steps to integrate their infrastructure, tariff regimes, and logistical chains. By 2007, trade among TRACECA members surpassed $40 billion, while their combined trade with the EU reached $290 billion.[168] Seventy percent of that trade was accounted for by oil, with most of it transiting along the Azerbaijani–Georgian segment of the corridor. Azerbaijan and Georgia are the two biggest beneficiaries of TRACECA. The corridor has also been beneficial for the hydrocarbon-exporting states, Kazakhstan and Turkmenistan. Overall, the limited non-energy export base of most of the members, coupled with obstacles related to border delays and controls, custom offices, and corruption, have limited TRACECA's potential to emerge as a major trade corridor. Nonetheless, with decreasing oil prices and shrinking profits from the oil sector, Azerbaijan has intensified efforts to diversify its economy and revive TRACECA and, especially, to strengthen transportation links with Central Asian states. In January 2015, the working group of the Coordination Committee of the Trans-Caspian International Transport Route (TITR) met in Baku and reached an agreement to intensify container service on its China–Kazakhstan–Azerbaijan–Georgia–Turkey route.[169] Azerbaijani authorities believe that by 2020, between 300,000 and 400,000 containers could be transported on the route, which would create billions of dollars for its participants. From this perspective, Azerbaijan needs a great deal of economic support from the EU, especially investments into the non-oil sector. Such investments would allow Baku to successfully diversify its economy in the face of volatile oil prices. Moreover, the EU's help in promoting Azerbaijan's export to EU countries could be crucial to assist Azerbaijan in solving its economic issues.[170]

168 Taleh Ziyadov, *Azerbaijan as a Regional Hub in Central Eurasia*, Baku: ADA University Press, 2012.

169 Eva Grey, "Can the Trans-Caspian Route Deliver the Next Freight Revolution?", *Railway Technology*, 4 November 2015, accessed 02.08.2018, http://www.railway-technology.com/features /featurecan-the-trans-caspian-route-deliver-the-next-freight-revolution-4684339/.

170 Anar Valiyev, "Can Azerbaijan Revive the Silk Road?" PONARS Eurasia Policy Memo No. 382, August 2015, accessed October 3, 2019 http://www.ponarseurasia.org/memo/can -azerbaijan-revive-silk-road.

Cultural Ties and Building European Identity
in Azerbaijan through Mega-Events

Although Azerbaijanis often declare their European identity, the question of the country's status in Europe has never been settled. Just as hundreds of years ago during the period of the first republic (1918–1920), Azerbaijanis are still struggling with this question.[171] Since independence, Azerbaijan has been unable to identify itself decisively with any particular part of the world.[172] Identification with the Islamic world was denied from the beginning, because of widespread Azerbaijani perceptions of its backwardness and the secular nature of the country's establishment and the majority of its population. European, or so-called Western, identity was the most attractive idea among the Azerbaijani establishment and people. For the last decade, the Azerbaijani government has used various strategies to reinforce European identity and to bring Azerbaijanis closer to European values. In 2013, the EU—the major exponent of European values—had modest level of support among the Azerbaijani people, with around 30% trusting the EU, while 37% expressed neutral feelings. Around 30% of people surveyed did not trust the EU, which was seen as evidence of the the scepticism of European values among Azerbaijanis.[173] Another survey conducted in May of 2017 showed surprising results.[174] According to this, almost every second Azerbaijani citizen (47%) takes a very or fairly positive view of the EU, compared to 9% of the population who are negatively disposed towards the Union. The majority of Azerbaijanis strongly believe that the EU represents

171 Anar Valiyev, "First European Olympic Games in Baku: New Articulation of Azerbaijani Identity?", in Andrey Makarychev and Alexandra Yatsyk (eds.) *2016: Mega Events in Post–Soviet Eurasia: Shifting Borderlines of Inclusion and Exclusion*, New York: Palgrave Macmillan, 2016, 131-149.

172 Svante Cornell, *Azerbaijan since Independence*. New York: M.E. Sharpe, 2011; EU Neighbourhood Survey, 2017, accessed 20.07.2018, https://www.euneighbours.eu/en/east/stay-informed /publications/opinion-survey-2017-azerbaijan.

173 Caucasus Barometer, "Public Opinion Survey Dataset. Trust Toward EU", 2013, http: //caucasusbarometer.org/en/cb-az/TRUSTEU/, accessed 14.08.2018.

174 Between March and May 2017, a second wave of annual surveys was carried out across the six Eastern Partner countries (Armenia, Azerbaijan, Belarus, Georgia, Moldova and Ukraine). The research was conducted within the framework of the EU-funded "OPEN Neighbourhood — Communicating for a stronger partnership: connecting with citizens across the Eastern Neighbourhood" ('EU NEIGHBOURS east') project. As part of the opinion polling strategy, the purpose of the annual surveys is to investigate the opinion and the level of information that citizens of the EaP countries have about the EU in general and, in particular, about EU-funded cooperation and development programmes/projects. In order to monitor changes over time, the surveys are being carried out annually from 2016 until 2019.

such values as human rights (overall, 81% of people share this belief), freedom of speech, democracy and the rule of law (each 80%), freedom of the media and economic prosperity (each 79%), equality and social justice, individual freedom, and honesty and transparency (each 74%). The European Union (and by extension Europe as a region) seems to be the most trusted foreign institution in Azerbaijan: half of the population tend to trust the EU (51%), while just over one third tend to trust both the UN (35%) and NATO (32%). By contrast, only a quarter trust the Russian-led EEU (26%).[175]

These results show a significant change in the perception of Europe among Azerbaijanis. It is believed that this shift is in response to the government's actions, as much as the will of the people. Moreover, such a change in perception has definitely affected the Azerbaijanis' sense of identity and their desire to belong to Europe. Since the disintegration of the Soviet Union, the country has undergone a tremendous transformation. In this context, demographic trends for the last decade have been quite favourable to the development of country, with a constant increase in the population due to a high birth rate. The economy of the country has boomed for the last twenty years. Much of Azerbaijan's economic success and prosperity is explained by its oil reserves. Oil prices have increased during the last decade, and oil and gas production has dramatically increased. As a result, the GDP per capita also grew to €3,411 in 2009. High oil revenues allowed Azerbaijan's GDP per capita to reach 54.3 percent of the average of ten EU countries (Latvia, Lithuania, Estonia, Czech Republic, Poland, Hungary, Slovenia, Slovakia, Romania, and Bulgaria). A windfall of oil revenue spurred the Azerbaijani government's initiative to spend a large amount of the profits on infrastructure projects, such as roads, bridges, and city beautification, as well as the hosting of mega-events. There were several reasons for striving for mega-events, and one of them was to boost and reinforce the image of European identity of Azerbaijan.[176] Cities competed for the honour of hosting various sporting events throughout the twentieth century, in order to benefit from the development connected with sports that has inspired the creation of cultural and leisure capital and reinforced place promotion

---

175 EU Neighborhood East, "Annual Survey Report – Azerbaijan, 2018", June 2018, https://www.euneighbours.eu/sites/default/files/publications/2018-07/EU%20NEIGBOURS%20east_AnnualSurvey2018report_AZERBAIJAN.pdf Retrieved on August 1, 2019.

176 Anar Valiyev, "Azerbaijan's Economic Model and Its Development since Independence", *in South Caucasus: 20 Years of Independence,* Friedrich-Ebert-Stiftung, 2011, 218-239.

and consumption-based economic development.[177] [178] [179] Seoul, Barcelona, London, Moscow, and Sochi in particular used large-scale sports events not only to advance economic development, but also to add themselves to the list of world-class cities. Although such development often tends to absorb a disproportionate share of resources, which hypothetically might go to other projects or places in the city, a number of developing cities continue to promote this cultural dimension and position cities as "places to play."[180] As the literature suggests,[181] one-time mega-events like the Olympic Games are large-scale spectacular productions which increasingly comprise advertising, entertainment, TV, and other mass media to stimulate consumer demand and tourism-oriented development. However, in Baku's case, these mega-events were used also to boast its European identity.

One of the first chances to boost the Eurocentric identity, as well as to build an image of Azerbaijan in Europe, was presented when the country won the 2011 Eurovision Song Contest. In accordance with the rules of the competition, Baku was expected to host the following year's event. Initially, Baku was not ready to do so. The city lacked a major venue in which to hold it, and the absence of infrastructure facility was also an issue. Baku subsequently invested hundreds of millions of dollars in the event, most of which was spent on infrastructure projects. In just nine months, the government built and opened Crystal Hall, a new convention centre to hold the song contest. Moreover, the government spent up to $600 million overall for additional projects associated with beautification and city development, while the direct cost for organisation of the event totalled only $34.3 million. Eurovision was the first event to put Baku and Azerbaijan at the centre of European culture. While for many Europeans, the Eurovision Song Contest is considered a common type of event, for Azerbaijan—which joined the contest just three years earlier—the country's victory and ability to host the subsequent event became

---

177 P. Bourdieu, "The Forms of Capital", in *Education: Culture Economy Society*, ed. A.H. Halsey, H. Lauder, P. Brown, and A.S. Wells. Oxford: Oxford University Press, 1997.

178 C. Euchner, "Tourism and Sports: The Serious Competition for Play", in *The Tourist City*, ed. D.R. Judd and S. Fainstein. New Haven: Yale University Press, 1999.

179 A. Gospodini, "Portraying, Classifying and Understanding the Emerging Landscapes in the Post-Industrial City", *Cities* 23 (5), 2006: 311–330.

180 P. Eisinger, "The Politics of Bread and Circuses: Building the City for the Visitor Class", *Urban Affairs Review*, 35, 2000: 316–333.

181 K. F. Gotham, "Theorizing Urban Spectacles: Festivals, Tourism and the Transformation of Urban Space", *City*, 9 (2) 2005: 225–246.

a kind of test of Europeanness. It was the first time Azerbaijan was able to associate itself symbolically with the rest of Europe.

The majority of the population was thrilled with this symbolic association. Moreover, according to an independent NGO, the Internet Forum of Azerbaijan, searches for Azerbaijan in Google increased eight-fold during the month following the 2011 song competition victory, while searches for Baku as a destination doubled. Meanwhile, interest in Azerbaijan multiplied by over forty on TripAdvisor. Finally, Baku's role in hosting the Eurovision in May of 2012 put Azerbaijan into a group of the ten most popular internet searches of May.[182] Beyond this high-level visibility, Eurovision had a marked impact on the self-identification of the Azerbaijani population, and especially the political and cultural establishment. For the first time, the Azerbaijani population was able to actually "live" in a European cultural milieu. For many people, it was fundamental in causing them to reappraise their roots in Europe while maintaining national customs and values.[183] The opening and closing ceremonies of the song contest featured themes from Azerbaijani culture and traditions, while the rest of the show represented wider European traditions. Azerbaijan's hosting of the Eurovision Song Contest in 2012 was the apex of the pro-European drive of its government, Enabling the country to be brought to the attention of Europe, while bringing part of Europe to Baku.

After the success of Eurovision and the hosting of some other events of regional significance, the Azerbaijani authorities felt the country was ready to host a larger event on an international scale. Consequently, Azerbaijan entered a bid to host the 2020 Olympic Games. Based on initial studies that estimated the hosting cost at $20 billion, the authorities suggested that oil revenues and private investment could finance it. By the time of the bid, Azerbaijan had already built thirteen new sporting complexes to bolster Baku's candidacy, with twenty-three additional buildings scheduled by 2014. However, in 2012, Baku lost its Olympic bid to Tokyo. Thus, the country shifted its strategy towards attracting smaller-scale or second-tier events, ostensibly with the aim of improving the city's portfolio for another Olympic bid in 2024 (which subsequently was also unsuccessful). On 8 December 2012, members of the 41st General Assembly of the European Olympic Committee (EOC) in Rome

---

182 Murad Ismayilov, "State, Identity, and the Politics of Music: Eurovision and Nation-Building in Azerbaijan', *Nationalities Papers*, 40 (6), 2012: 833-851.
183 Ibid.

decided to hold the first ever European Games, with Baku awarded the rights to host the inaugural event in 2015. The decision was made as a result of secret balloting, where of 48 votes cast, 38 were in favour, 8 against, and 2 abstained. EOC President Patrick Hickey stated after the voting: "We stand at the origins of one of the greatest events in the sport history in Europe. I am proud to say: the first European Games will be held in 2015 in Baku. Our long-awaited baby has been finally born. And now we'll look after him carefully and raise it to make everything at top notch in the beautiful city of Baku. And most importantly, that it was only the beginning—the first page of a multiyear, full and vibrant life of European Games."[184] It was interesting that Azerbaijan was one of the major proponents for the establishment of an event of this kind, and calling it the European Games helped Azerbaijan to promote itself once again as a part of Europe. Azad Rahimov, Minister of Youth and Sports, declared after the Games: "It is very important for a country that gained independence only 23 years ago to position itself on the map of Europe as a European country. Very often the question [is asked,] 'Where is Azerbaijan?' After the Eurovision Song Contest and after the European Games, most people will know the answer.[185]

Planners were highly focused on preparing for the 2015 European Games, which were expected to bring six thousand athletes from forty-nine countries to Baku. The European Games featured up to twenty sports, including fifteen Summer Olympic and two non-Olympic ones. "This is going to be the most fantastic show ever staged in Azerbaijan, one that will make the Eurovision Song Contest seem like a small, local event," the Chief Operating Officer of the Baku European Games Operations Committee (BEGOC), Simon Clegg, stated. Attracting high-quality athletes was an important first step, Clegg contended, and it was accomplished by ensuring that sixteen of the twenty participating sports could use the Baku Games as a qualifying or ranking event for the Rio 2016 Summer Olympics. Baku wanted to ensure the Games would be broadcast all over the world, from Australia to South America. The

184 Anar Valiyev, "First European Olympic Games in Baku: New Articulation of Azerbaijani Identity?", in Andrey Makarychev and Alexandra Yatsyk (eds.), *2016: Mega Events in Post–Soviet Eurasia: Shifting Borderlines of Inclusion and Exclusion*, New York: Palgrave Macmillan, 2016, 131-149.
185 Georgi Gotev, "Minister: After The Baku Games, Azerbaijan Will Be An Even More Popular Destination", *Euroactive.com*, 25 May 2015, accessed 03.10.2019, https://www.euractiv.com/section/sports/interview/minister-after-the-baku-games-azerbaijan-will-be-an-even-more-popular-destination/.

government altered its immigration policy, to waive the visa requirement for all participating athletes and officials in possession of an accreditation card. In addition, all foreign spectators only received visas upon arrival based on proof of purchase of tickets. Some six thousand athletes and three thousand officials from the National Olympic Committees of Europe participated in the Games, which, as Clegg believed, became the "second most important event in the history of Azerbaijan after the signing of the contract of the century in 1994," referring to the deal with an international consortium to develop the giant Azeri–Chirag–Gunashli oilfields. It was estimated that 1,600 staff hired by BEGOC and twelve thousand volunteers would walk away with new skills and an appetite for volunteering in sporting and other types of events.

Initial estimates placed the cost of the 2015 European Games at around $1 billion, including the construction of a $720-million Olympic Stadium, which was inaugurated in June 2011 by Azerbaijan's President Aliyev, together with presidents of FIFA, Sepp Blatter, and UEFA, Michel Platini.[186] The construction was finished by May 2015, with a seating capacity of 65,000.[187] Within the stadium precinct, there are warm-up and training facilities for athletes that include seating for up to two thousand spectators, parklands and parking facilities, as well as a new Athletes Village. Meanwhile, numerous other facilities were constructed to support this event, including thirteen newly constructed, luxurious buildings for five thousand athletes. Although preparations have concentrated on new construction, planners intend to temporarily repurpose some older Soviet-era structures, as well as the recently-built Crystal Hall.

For Baku, the major concern has been to ensure international recognition and the maintenance of a good image. The appointment of Dimitris Papaioannou, the artistic director of the Athens 2004 Olympic Games ceremonies, to a similar position at the Baku 2015 opening ceremony speaks volumes about the intent to stage a show to remember. To impress visitors, it is essential that a host city has all the attributes of major cities: an international airport, a signature building designed by prominent architects, and other impressive buildings and cultural complexes.[188] By

186 Trend.az, "FIFA, UEFA Presidents Inaugurate New Stadium in Baku", 6 June 2011.
187 Baku European Games Operation Committee, 2014, accessed 02.05. 2018, http://www.baku2015.com/en/.
188 Andrew Jonas and David Wilson (eds.), *The Urban Growth Machine*, Albany: State University of New York University Press, 1999.

the end of 2014, most of these attributes had been built. The newly inaugurated terminal at Baku airport is a masterpiece of architecture: constructed in a triangular shape with rounded off angles, it was designed to host about three million passengers each year. Several other magnificent new buildings have been constructed in Baku. The SOCAR Tower—the tallest building in Baku and the entire Caucasus—became home to the State Oil Company in 2015. The opening ceremony of the European Games, held at the new Olympic stadium, in the opinion of local media commentators, exceeded all expectations. Baku spent around $100 million for the show, which even included bringing Lady Gaga to sing the John Lennon song "Imagine." Traditional music and about two thousand female dancers and artists set the stage for the flame-lighting ceremony, which officially opened the Games, followed by an exposition dedicated to the literary writing of the famous twelfth-century Azerbaijani poet, Nizami Ganjavi. Another $140 million was spent on the closing ceremony that concluded the seventeen-day event. The presidents of Russia and Turkey, as well as several other former Soviet republics, attended the event. The European Games were successful for Baku since they presented evidence of Azerbaijan's modernity and its rise to international prominence. Officials claimed that the Games were a promotional opportunity for Azerbaijan, a nation that was still little-known to many people around the world. The broadcasting rights for the Games were sold to European, US, and Canadian companies, which also transmitted the event to the Middle East and North Africa. 447 million households in China were able to watch through CCTV, as well as 56 million households in Japan and 30 million households in India.

The success of the European Games allowed Baku to secure other international events. Azerbaijan went on to host the Chess Olympiad in 2016 and the Islamic Solidarity Games in 2017. Even before the European Games, Azerbaijan confirmed it would be bringing the Formula 1 European Grand Prix to Baku from July 2016. For this event, Hermann Tilke's architectural firm produced an urban highway in the city centre. As the host of a Formula 1 event, Baku stands alongside Monaco, Singapore, and other major cities. The organisers arranged that, during the race, the cars move in parallel with the boulevards and make a tour of the Old City, a national historical and architectural centre that is considered the most ancient part of Baku and a UNESCO World Heritage Site. Azad Rahimov spoke of the country's location at the crossroads of Eastern Europe and Western Asia as a new "frontier": "Azerbaijan is a modern European country that has established a reputation as a centre of sporting excellence. The deal to bring Formula 1 racing to Baku is a very significant new chapter in our ongoing success to attract the world's largest sporting events to our country."[189]

Conclusion and Recommendations

It is too early to predict the future direction of Azerbaijan's foreign policy with regard to the EU. However, it is hard to imagine that Azerbaijan will give up its focus on European development. Most of the strategic projects in Azerbaijan are primarily connected with Europe. The Baku–Tbilisi–Ceyhan oil pipeline; the Trans Anatolian Natural Gas Pipeline; the transport corridor from Central Asia to Europe; and many other projects require European involvement. The Azerbaijani leadership would not easily be able or willing to sever relations with the EU. Furthermore, despite the harsh rhetoric and a halt on integration, the cultural image of Europe in Azerbaijan remains largely positive, and many Azerbaijanis are frequent travellers to the EU, especially after the visa facilitation agreement.

Meanwhile, the soft power of Europe in Azerbaijan should not be underestimated. Besides the technological advances, entertainment industry, and even travel preferences, the European education system is a major destination for Azerbaijani students who wish to continue their education abroad. Thousands of Azerbaijani students are currently studying in Europe, with many given this opportunity through Erasmus and other EU programmes. Many graduates of EU universities have returned to find jobs in the Azerbaijani government. Establishing joint educational programmes with Azerbaijani universities, or creating new programmes to educate Azerbaijani youth, could be great stimulus and further improve the positive image of the EU. In addition to education, the West should pay specific attention to the media space of the region. Today, most of the information Azerbaijanis receive is via local, Russian, or Turkish sources—this deprives people of unbiased information and boosts Russian influence in particular. The establishment of new TV channels within the country, or news services in the Azerbaijani language, would allow local populations to obtain first-hand information,

---

189 Andrew Benson, "Azerbaijan to Hold Formula 1 Race on Baku Street Sircuit in 2016", *BBC*, 25 July 2014, accessed 14.05.2018, http://www.bbc.com/sport/0/formula1/28483319.

bypassing these external sources. Azerbaijan today understands that the country's future lies in greater integration with the EU. Sooner or later, both sides will agree to deeper cooperation.

When attempting to predict Azerbaijan's future relations with the EU, one must take several factors into consideration: the EU's active policy in Azerbaijan; EU–Turkish relations; and EU–Russian relations. The EU's recent decision to grant visa-free regimes to Georgia and Ukraine has been encouraging for the Azerbaijani public. The average citizen was able to see the benefits of cooperation with EU, especially considering that there is a significant ethnic Azerbaijani minority in Georgia who are now able to travel to the Schengen area without visas. At the same time, the public was frustrated that such an agreement was not reached with Azerbaijan. If, in the future, the EU seeks to appeal to the Azerbaijani people and extend its soft power in the country, it should work with the government on various issues separately, rather than as a single package. For example, a visa-free agreement could be negotiated independently from other issues that raise more troubling questions for the Azerbaijani government. Next, the deterioration of EU–Turkish relations may also affect Azerbaijani perceptions of the Union, as Turkey had been a model for the Azerbaijani establishment as well as a long-term partner. Finally, the continued "cold war" between Russia and the West, and the Russian perception of the South Caucasus as a frontier in that struggle, will continue to present an obstacle to Azerbaijan's integration with the EU. Without an active EU policy towards the region, Azerbaijan will not be able to overcome these obstacles and will remain in limbo, vulnerable to both external and domestic threats.

This chapter is written with the support of the GCRF UKRI COMPASS project 2017–21 (ES/P010849/1), led by the University of Kent.

CHAPTER 4
Azerbaijan's Place in West-Central Eurasian Energy Security

Robert M. Cutler

Introduction

This chapter is a retrospective evaluation and extension of a previous review-and-prospect work, published in 2012 but completed two years earlier, in a volume dedicated to previewing the South Caucasus in 2021.[190] Since we are now arriving at the end of the 2010s, such an evaluation seems proper. The earlier work, completed at a time when the Nabucco Pipeline still seemed a viable export option, comprised six sections, which I will first summarise briefly. Aside from this summary, the material here is new.

The first section of the original study reviewed three centuries of international politics in what I will now call Greater Turco-Caucasia, with a focus on Russian–Turkish relations. The second section focused more closely on the region's energy geopolitics in the 1990s and 2000s. It distinguished between Greater Central Asian and what I then called Greater Southwest Asian geoeconomic energy complexes. Why I now prefer the term "Greater Turco-Caucasia" to "Greater Southwest Asia" is explained below. Also, the title of the present chapter reflects the fact that, since the original publication, the Greater Central Asian hydrocarbon energy complex (HEC) has been extended to become the East Central Eurasian HEC, while what was the Greater Turco-Caucasian HEC has extended

---

190 Robert M. Cutler, "Azerbaijan's Place in Euro-Caspian Energy Security", in Glen Howard and Fariz Izmailzade (eds.), *Oil, Democracy and Geopolitics*, London: Routledge, 2012, 107–30.

itself to become the West Central Eurasian HEC. All these terms are briefly defined below.

The third section of the original chapter focused attention on the development Azerbaijan's offshore Shah Deniz gas field, the EU-promoted Nabucco gas pipeline project, and Nabucco's competitors, notably (but not only) Russia's South Stream project. The fourth section then analysed the possibility of a Trans-Caspian Gas Pipeline (TCGP) from Turkmenistan to Azerbaijan. It discussed the history of the project in the late 1990s, various Azerbaijani–Turkmen disagreements, the delimitation of offshore national sectors in the Caspian Sea, and the development and expansion of Kazakhstan's Kashagan and Karachaganak projects. It noted that the TCGP would be an essential geoeconomic link, connecting Greater Central Asia to what I then called Greater Southwest Asia (and which, to repeat, I here call, more accurately, Greater Turco-Caucasia).

The fifth section of the original chapter looked at such Black Sea projects, in the then near future, as the Azerbaijan–Georgia–Romania Interconnector (AGRI), Russia's Blue Stream Pipeline project, the EU's overall Southern Gas Corridor (SGC) programme, and the White Stream Pipeline project under the Black Sea. It then considered this examination in the context of the Russo-Turkish energy entente described in the chapter's first two sections, concluding correctly that the "Putin–Erdogan entente will not be confined to energy and other economic matters."[191] The final section of that earlier chapter recapitulated the significance of the intensive survey of then-ongoing developments, from the perspectives of the three-century and two-decade perspectives set out at the start.

This present chapter develops the points made principally in the fourth, but also in the fifth, section of the earlier work. It underlines how the Greater Turco-Caucasian HEC (defined below) has been knit together with the Greater Central Asian HEC. This evolution continues at present, expanding the former into the West Central Eurasian HEC and the latter into the East Central Eurasian HEC, which now intersect. In that evolution, the TCGP project plays a crucial role.

The conclusions of the original study, as well as the framework outlined below, hold up well. In the original chapter, I wrote that Azerbaijan is "the crucible where questions concerning the future structure of geo-economic relations in Eurasia... are today being resolved." This has not changed. The country's significance arises not only from "its

---

191 Ibid., 126-27.

[own] natural energy resources [both also] from its irreplaceable role as a bridge from Central Asia and [from] the Caspian Sea basin to the Black Sea basin and Europe."[192] Progress in implementing the TCGP project, with Azerbaijan's participation, only underlines more strongly this proposition.

Developments since publication of the original work have created need for some conceptual and terminological clarification. As mentioned, I was never happy with the "Greater Southwest Asia" category. It could easily have been taken to include the Arabian Peninsula and even the Levant: as the US military-strategic use of the term "Southwest Asia" in fact does. Now I consider that it should be called "Greater Turco-Caucasia," which is more descriptive and more accurate. Let me briefly explain the significance. Ismailov defines the North Caucasus as comprising a part of the Southern Federal District of the Russian Federation, and in particular: two territories, two regions, and one republic in the "Piedmont Area;" and seven republics in the "Mountainous Area." (This region notably stretches as far north as the Russian oil port of Novorossiisk on the Black Sea, although it does not include the pipeline of the Caspian Pipeline Corporation originating in Kazakhstan; and still it includes the oil pipeline that in the 1990s ran from Baku through Chechnya, as well as its diversion through Dagestan after war broke out in Chechnya.) What is now generally called the South Caucasus, Ismailov calls the "Central Caucasus." What he calls the "South Caucasus" includes seven provinces in northeastern Turkey and six provinces in northwestern Iran.[193] In order to avoid confusion, I retain the term "South Caucasus" to refer to Azerbaijan, Armenia, and Georgia. What he calls the South Caucasus, I refer to as the "Southernmost Caucasus." Thus, here the North, South, and Southernmost Caucasus comprise "the Caucasus".

I use the term "Turco-Caucasia" to signify the geoeconomic enlargement of this region through the implementation of oil and gas exploitation and transmission projects, notably but not only the Baku–Tbilisi–Ceyhan (BTC) Oil Pipeline from the Azerbaijani offshore Azeri–Chirag–Guneshli oil deposit. "Turco-Caucasia" includes that part of the Anatolian Peninsula to the east of the BTC Pipeline, as well as northern Iraq, including the Kirkuk–Ceyhan Pipeline, and that larger

---

192 Ibid., 107.
193 Eldar Ismailov, "The Main Parameters of the Caucasian Economic Space", in Eldar Ismailov and Vladimer Papava, *The Central Caucasus: Essays on Geopolitical Economy,* Luleå, Sweden: CA&CC Press, 2006, 59-83.

part of northern Iran populated in the majority by ethnic Azerbaijanis. "Greater Turco-Caucasia" in turn signifies the geoeconomic evolution of this region to a still greater scale, including the whole of the Anatolian Peninsula, the rest of which is adjoined to Turco-Caucasia by the extension of the Trans Anatolian Natural Gas Pipeline (TANAP). It extends also further south in Iraq beyond the Kirkuk–Ceyhan line, as well as comprehending certain Iranian provinces, in the north and northwest, where Turkic peoples are not just in the majority but also in the minority.

The "Hydrocarbon Energy Complex" as Unit for Analysis

By "hydrocarbon energy complex" (HEC), I mean a conceptual construct of a region that is unified by energy flows typically institutionalised by oil and gas pipelines. It is considered as a geoeconomic unit for analysis. The adjective "geoeconomic" focuses attention on (1) how the "international structure" constrains national choices about energy resource development without uniquely determining them; (2) how those choices feed back into the structuration of regional international systems; and (3) how these latter constellations themselves reconfigure "system-level" international structures. This geoeconomic HEC approach considers pipeline networks (oil and gas transmission systems) to be complex adaptive systems, executed by human agency, that transform their human and physical economic, political, financial, and ideological environments.[194] These environments reciprocally contribute to the structuring and evolutionary restructuring of HECs, not excluding their overlap and merger.

Pipeline networks and their associated social systems therefore participate in the geopolitical configuration and reconfiguration of the territories where hydrocarbon energy is produced, transmitted, and consumed. They can alter inherited balance of power geopolitical patterns by unifying elements of adjacent geoeconomic subregions in new ways. They frequently represent cooperative international ententes, sometimes verging on de facto political alliances. They can transform international regions and promote interregional restructuring from the bottom up.

---

194 For further explanation, see Robert M. Cutler, "Russia, Kazakhstan, and Their National Oil Companies", in M,P. Amineh and Y. Guang (eds.), *Geopolitical Economy of Energy and Environment: China and the European Union,* Leiden–Boston: Brill, 2017, 231–271.

This was most evident in the circum-Caspian littoral regions in the 1990s and early 2000s.

HECs are defined following the ontological premise of the study of complex systems, namely that theoretical entities (such as HECs) do not represent real entities unless the phenomena follow the hypotheses in every detail. Epistemologically, this represents an application of empirically motivated conventionalism: a construct is justified because it permits interpretation in some way of known facts, on the basis of concepts, and incorporates principles for the logical ordering things as yet to be discovered. The order is never complete, for there are always recalcitrant phenomena: these do not invalidate the chosen scheme but, rather, they challenge the observer to rebuild the phenomena analytically until they fit into it. This explanation shows that HECs also evolve and why, as complex systems, they can overlap and merge in the course of their evolution.

Recent geoeconomic trends, in retrospect somehow ineluctable but not predetermined, argue strongly that the Greater Central Asia region, and its HEC in particular, has expanded into a East Central Eurasian HEC, with the China–Kazakhstan–Russia energy triangle as its basis. Meanwhile, the Greater Turco-Caucasian HEC has expanded into a West Central Eurasian HEC, still based upon the Azerbaijan–Russia–Turkey energy triangle set out in the original study. Although I have consistently used a category of "Central Eurasia" for over a decade,[195] the evolution of eastern and western HECs within it, and particularly their emergent interconnections, is not a manifestation of natural law. That is because human agency intervenes and has prevented certain other tendencies of energy geoeconomic evolution over this same period of time. As such, the present evolution of Eurasian energy geoeconomics is in fact not wholly expected, although it is aesthetically pleasing and its analysis as a phenomenon is empirically justified.

The name "Central Eurasia" was sometimes used in the 1990s as a shorthand for the fifteen former Soviet republics together, but this usage has faded away. I adopt the ethnographic and cultural definition from the founding statement of purpose of the Central Eurasian Studies Society, that it includes "Turkic, Mongolian, Iranian, Caucasian, Tibetan and other peoples[, and] extends from the Black Sea region, the Crimea,

---

195 See, for example, Robert M. Cutler, "U.S.-Russian Strategic-Military Relations in Central Asia", *Perspectives on Global Development and Technology*, 6 (1-3), 2007: 109-125.

and the Caucasus in the west, through the Middle Volga region, Central Asia and Afghanistan, and on to Siberia, Mongolia and Tibet in the east."[196] To clarify the "Black Sea region," which appears in that definition, I adopt the EU's characterisation of the area as "stretch[ing] from Romania and Bulgaria, through northern Turkey and on to Georgia," but including only "a thin coastal strip some 20–60 km wide" within the EU itself, including the Danube Delta.[197]

The collapse of the Soviet Union did not assure the geoeconomic consolidation of Central Eurasia, but the conditions for that consolidation were soon established. This occurred thanks to the confluence of international financial and industrial interests in the region's energy resources, the political will of the United States (the only remaining superpower), and the freedom and rapidity of networked information exchanges made possible by the internet.

A "Complex-Scientific" Approach

The approach employed here is "complex-scientific," i.e., based in the science of the study of complex systems. A complex system is a system having multiple interacting components, of which the overall behaviour cannot be inferred simply from that of the components. The complex--scientific approach to energy geoeconomics embeds three distinctive methods and tools of analysis. They are emergent coherence, energy triangles, and nestedness.

1. "Emergent coherence" is a shorthand for a particular type of complex-scientific social-system evolution, the emergence–autopoiesis–coherence (EAC) cycle.[198] "Emergence" and "coherence" are intermediated by "autopoiesis," literally meaning "self-creation" or "self-production." Autopoietic dynamics explain the extension of

---

196 This phrase does not appear on the organisation's new website <http://www.centraleurasia.org>. It is, however, archived at <http://web.archive.org/web/20030429160511fw_/http://cess.fas.harvard.edu:80/CESSpg_org_info.html> and <http://archive.is/l701c> under the tab "About CESS | Statement of Purpose". These URLs, and all others cited here, are verified as of 31 July 2018 unless otherwise noted.

197 European Commission, "Black Sea Region", accessed 31.07.2018, http://ec.europa.eu/environment/nature/natura2000/biogeog_regions/blacksea/index_en.htm.

198 Robert M. Cutler, "The Paradox of Intentional Emergent Coherence: Organization and Decision in a Complex World", *Journal of the Washington Academy of Sciences,* 92 (4), 2007:, 9–27; Robert M. Cutler and Alexander von Lingen, "An Evolutionary Phenomenology of Resilience", *Kybernetes* (August 2018), <https://doi.org/10.1108/K-11-2017-0460>.

hydrocarbon energy pipeline networks out from the Caspian Sea basin to Europe and China. A potential pipeline project first emerges and then alters its form as necessary through the working of the (evolutionary) principle of variation. Such altered forms then either survive (such as the evolution of the Baku–Supsa Oil Pipeline into Baku–Tbilisi–Ceyhan) or fail to survive (for instance, the evolution of the Nabucco project into the Nabucco-West variant, which was subsequently abandoned). The surviving pipeline projects are those that have cohered, through the (evolutionary) principle of selection, in a manner best adapted to their environment.

2. The use of "energy triangles" as the constitutive bases of difference HECs highlights the fact that the dynamics of triads differ qualitatively from any aggregation or iteration of bilateral or dyadic relations. The Baku–Tbilisi–Ceyhan Oil Pipeline—the first trilateral project implemented in the history of the global hydrocarbon industry—cannot be reduced to an aggregation of bilateral Azerbaijani–Georgian, Azerbaijani–Turkish, and Georgian–Turkish relations. Such multilateral arrangements, sometimes with even more numerous partners, have now become the norm throughout European and Eurasian geoeconomics. This method of triangles may be extended to higher orders of multilateral relations. Quadrilateral relations, for example, may be constituted as a series of non-intersecting, contiguous triangles.

3. "Nestedness," the third complex-scientific principle, highlights the fact that every HEC is "nested" within various scales of analysis. As suggested above, Greater Central Asia nests Central Asia and is nested within Central Eurasia as its eastern component. Greater Turco-Caucasia nests Turco-Caucasia and is nested within Central Eurasia as its western component.[199] In addition, nested within each chronological phase of emergence, autopoiesis, and coherence, it may be possible to distinguish subphases of emergence, autopoiesis, and coherence. Likewise, a cyle comprising phases of emergence, autopoiesis, and coherence may itself be nested within a "super-phase" that may itself represent meta-emergence, meta-autopoiesis, or meta-coherence on an extended scale.

---

199 For a broader discussion of this point, see Robert M. Cutler, "The Complexity of Central Eurasia", *Central Eurasian Studies Review,* 3 (1), 2004: 2–3.

The Energy Geoeconomic Merging of East and West Central Eurasia: Background to Current Developments

In retrospect, it is possible to see that Central Eurasia's geoeconomic consolidation grew out of the independent consolidation, first of Greater Central Asia and of Greater Turco-Caucasia, and second out of their knitting-together with one another, as the former transformed into East Central Eurasia and the latter into West Central Eurasia.

Immediately after the fall of the Soviet Union, these geoeconomic regions of Turco-Caucasia and Central Asia were not connected by international energy flows. Indeed, the separation of the South Caucasus from Soviet rule began already in the late 1980s, a half-decade before the Central Asian states were finally severed from the Russian rouble currency zone in 1992–1993. It was only around the years 2003–2004, with the geoeconomic enlargement of Central Asia into Greater Central Asia, and of Turco-Caucasia into Greater Turco-Caucasia, that movement began towards their merging together. The most obvious manifestations of this phenomenon were the unsuccessful attempt to implement the TCGP at that time and the successful implementation of the Caspian Pipeline Corporation (CPC) pipeline, enabling oil from Kazakhstan's Tengiz deposit to cross southern Russia to its Black Sea port of Novorossiisk (and subsidiary port of Tuapse).

The CPC pipeline was indeed a main artery of the geoeconomic enlargement of Central Asia into Greater Central Asia. Unsuccessful attempts at the further development of the Karachaganak gas deposit, which depends upon the Russian processing plant in Omsk, also played a role, albeit less significant. Likewise, the construction and entry into service of the Baku–Tbilisi–Ceyhan (BTC) oil pipeline, from Azerbaijan's offshore through Georgia to Turkey's East Mediterranean coast, which occurred in roughly the same time frame, was an important driving force in the geoeconomic enlargement of Turco-Caucasia into Greater Turco-Caucasia.

The BTC oil export pipeline, as well as Azerbaijani exports through Dagestan (replacing Chechnya) into the CPC route, were in evidence. Also, Kazakhstan's supergiant offshore strike at Kashagan raised the possibilities (not yet implemented) for gas exports under the Caspian Sea through the South Caucasus to Europe, as well as the Kazakhstan Caspian Transportation System (KCTS). This latter project still envisages bringing Kashagan oil onshore, constructing a pipeline inside Kazakhstan from Atyrau to Kuryk, then an undersea pipeline to

Azerbaijan, for Kashagan oil to enter the BTC for export to the world market.

Various projects on a larger scale, but which were not realised—such as the earlier planned development of Kazakhstan's offshore Kashagan gas deposit, as well as the intended extension of the Nabucco gas pipeline project into Central Asia—were pointers in the direction of the knitting-together of Greater Central Asia and Greater Turco-Caucasia, a process transforming them respectively into East and West Central Eurasia. The TCGP project, connecting up with the now-established Southern Gas Corridor, looks to accomplish that merger of the geoeconomic regions already extended respectively from Central Asia and Turco-Caucasia.

The first TCGP project, sponsored by the United States, fell apart in the late 1990s. A few years later, the EU decided to extend contacts with Central Asia to ensure the security of its own energy supply. The first concrete move in this direction was the 2004 Baku Initiative, based upon recommendations from a report by the Centre for European Policy Studies that was subsequently endorsed by a leading committee of the European Parliament. The 2007 Strategy for a New Partnership with Central Asia then followed, also prominently mentioning energy cooperation. Eventually, in 2011, the European Commission authorised that the European Union adopt a mandate (the first of its kind) to negotiate a legally binding treaty between the EU, Azerbaijan, and Turkmenistan, to build a "Trans Caspian Pipeline System."

Events since spring 2017 have greatly accelerated this development. In April 2017, the Georgian Oil and Gas Corporation acquired 10 percent of the TCGP promoter companies. In May, Georgia's prime minister Giorgi Kvirikashvili confirmed that Georgia was "working intensively on the project of transporting gas from Turkmenistan to Europe, the White Stream project, which brings new opportunities for the diversification of Europe's energy supply."[200] The White Stream project is the planned Georgia–Romania natural gas pipeline under the Black Sea, that would take gas from the TCGP's second string directly to EU territory. Through the first string, Turkmenistan's gas would enter southern Europe through the TANAP–TAP pipeline complex of the Southern Gas Corridor.

---

200 Government of Georgia, "Address of by [sic] H.E Giorgi Kvirikashvili, prime Minister of Georgia to the NATO Parliamentary Assembly", 29 May 2017, accessed 31.07.2018, http://gov.ge/index .php?lang_id=ENG&sec_id=463&info_id=61201.

The idea that gas from Europe's east should have two entry points to Europe arose during planning for the second attempt to build the TCGP, in the context of competition between the Nabucco and South Stream projects ten years ago. The European Coordinator's 2009 report on implementing the Caspian Development Corporation adopted this idea, even suggesting a continuation of the White Stream pipeline to Trieste, in order to secure different markets for both this and Nabucco.[201] The new, current TCGP project follows this idea by aiming at two entry points for Turkmenistan's gas to Europe: one for each of the pipeline's two strings.

More precisely, the TCGP's first string, carrying 16 billion cubic meters per year (bcm/y), would pass from Azerbaijan through the South Caucasus Pipeline (now being expanded from SCP to SCPx), then via Turkey's East–West TANAP to Greece, whence to Italy by way of the Trans Adriatic Pipeline (TAP). With comparatively modest incremental outlay, yielding excellent cost/benefit ratios, this system can handle gas from the TCGP, significantly enhancing the EU's advantages from the SGC.

The TCGP's second string, also for 16 bcm/y, would run under the Black Sea, costing less than the Turkish route and targeting a different market. The second string would satisfy the increasing import needs of Germany and its neighbours. Instead of entering Turkey and Greece, gas from the TCGP's second string would transit Georgia to the coast of the Black Sea, and via the White Stream pipeline to be laid beneath it, would land in Romania. From there, Turkmen gas would reach Central Europe by two routes.

The first route for gas from TCGP's second string, once ashore in EU territory (Constanţa, Romania), may utilise capacity from the Bulgaria–Romania–Hungary–Austria (BRUA) pipeline now under construction. Another intra-European route from Constanţa would have larger capacity. This second route would go north by reverse flow through the Trans-Balkan pipeline (after Gazprom's contracts with Romania and Ukraine expire in 2019), then through Ukraine's gas transmission system (GTS) for subsequent distribution to Poland, Austria, and (by the Bratstvo pipeline) Slovakia, Czechia, and Germany.

---

201 Jozias van Aartsen, "Activity Report, September 2007 – February 2009: Project of European Interest NG3", Brussels, 4 February 2009, accessed 31.07.2018, https://www.rijksoverheid.nl /binaries/rijksoverheid/documenten/rapporten/2009/03/27/1-activity-report/9059266-bijlage .pdf, now archived at https://zoek.officielebekendmakingen.nl/blg-12831.pdf.

European energy security policy reached a milestone in early June 2018 when TANAP was opened, running east–west across Turkey (1,850 kilometres) from the Georgian to the Greek border. It will carry, in the first instance, natural gas from Azerbaijan's Shah Deniz 2 offshore gas field in the Caspian Sea, which will reach TANAP through the already existing South Caucasus Pipeline.

The opening of the TANAP–TAP system thus also represents the formal opening of the SGC's first stage. But it is not expected that projected additional volumes will come from Azerbaijan any time soon. The best candidate to supply them is Turkmenistan. Therefore, the EU continues its active support of the TCGP project.

Technically, this project is easy, but politically, it has been difficult. The attempt led by American companies foundered twenty years ago, when Turkmenistan and Turkey, and then Turkmenistan and Azerbaijan, were unable to agree. While they were still discussing terms, the Russia–Turkey Blue Stream pipeline project took off, and the Shah Deniz project operator BP discovered that that deposit held mainly natural gas, rather than the crude oil that was expected. As a result, Azerbaijan helped to develop the SCP for the Turkish market without an export quota for Turkmenistan.

The leaders of Azerbaijan and Turkmenistan from that time passed from the scene a decade ago. The new leaders reconciled and gave indications of mutual accommodation , but even so, the TCGP was never built for a series of idiosyncratic reasons. Now that has changed. Gas from the TCGP's first string could reach Greece and possibly Italy for European distribution in 2022. Gas transiting the second string would then arrive in Romania as early as 2023.

Significance of Current Developments: Analytical Significance for Periodisation

Recall that the Greater Turco-Caucasian HEC grows into the West Central Eurasian HEC and the Greater Central Asian HEC grows into the East Central Eurasian HEC. Recall also that these enlargements permit these complexes to merge and grow into one another. How should the gradual evolution of this phenomenon be periodised? The West Central Eurasian and East Central Eurasian HECs together define—although not necessarily exhaustively—the Central Eurasian HEC, of which the periodisation may be split between its two original components.

As established in previously cited work, the first three phases of the evolution of what I now call the Greater Turco-Caucasian HEC were 1989–1994, 1995–2000, and 2001–2006; whereas the first three phases of the evolution of the Greater Central Asian HEC were 1995–2000, 2001–2006, and 2007–2012. This five-year offset is due to the fact that the "post-Soviet transition" began in the South Caucasus roughly five years earlier than in Central Asia. The civil wars in Georgia and the Azerbaijani–Armenian war over Nagorno-Karabakh all date from the mid- to late 1980s. By contrast, Central Asia was the last region of the USSR where the republics declared their independence. Kazakhstan was indeed the very last, four days after Russia.

Naturally, it appears prudent to split the difference between the Turco-Caucasian and Central Asian HECs in defining the first phase of the evolution of the general Central Eurasian HEC, an approach which is supported by the real history of the network. The first three phases of evolution of the Central Eurasian HEC then acquire the dates 1992–1997, 1998–2003, and 2004–2009.

As the Central Eurasian HEC's two components have grown together and increasingly intertwined from 1992 to 2009, it becomes appropriate to refer to the Greater Turco-Caucasian HEC as the Western Central Eurasian HEC, and to the Greater Central Asian HEC as the Eastern Central Eurasian HEC. In further evolution, one may observe the former enlarging to extend to southern Europe, for example, via the Southern Gas Corridor to Italy, and the latter to the Chinese seacoast and eastern Siberia. Subsequently, one may speculate that the Central Eurasian HEC will enlarge into a Greater Central Eurasian HEC.

These three phases complete one cycle of emergence, autopoiesis, and coherence. But then what follows? The principle of complex-scientific nestedness animating this geoeconomic analysis applies not only to space, but also to time. Therefore, the years 1992–2009 are conceived to represent, for the Central Eurasian HEC, a "metaphase" of meta-emergence, followed by metaphases of meta-autopoiesis (comprising another EAC cycle periodised as 2010–2015, 2016–2021, and prospectively 2022–2027). The projects entering into service during these years will be the defining axes of development for the entire energy production sector from Central Europe to Central Asia, for the whole half-century following the disintegration of the Soviet state. The final metaphase of meta-coherence then falls into the period 2028–2045. This is the schema that has guided this evaluation of the analysis of the earlier work, and which guides also the analysis of events since its composition—roughly the decade of the 2010s.

Practical Significance for the TCGP

In June 2017, the Council of the European Union reaffirmed the goal of extending the Southern Gas Corridor into Central Asia, "further promot[ing] the EU's multilateral and bilateral energy cooperation" with the countries there.[202] Later that month, Maroš Šefčovič, Vice President of the European Commission, welcomed Georgia's accession to the Energy Community and singled out its role in extending the Southern Gas Corridor to additional supply countries.[203] All these declarations set the stage for further developments in the region itself. In August 2017, the leaders of Azerbaijan and Turkmenistan signed for the first time an agreement to bring Caspian energy resources to Europe.[204]

In December 2017, Šefčovič again reaffirmed the TCGP as "an important, complementary element of the Southern Gas Corridor in order to connect the significant gas reserves of Central Asia to the European markets."[205] By the end of 2017, the TCGP was included among the EU's List of Projects of Common Interest, which qualified it for preferential financial regulatory treatment by European institutions.

Since March 2018, the European Commission is funding the Pre-FEED (Front-End Engineering and Design), Reconnaissance Surveys, and Strategic and Economic Evaluations of the TCGP.[206] All supposed obstacles to the planning and construction of the pipeline now appear to be fading, including the non-delimitation of the national subsea sectors of the Caspian Sea littoral states.

---

202 Council of the European Union, "Council Conclusions on the EU Strategy for Central Asia", Annex to "Outcome of Proceedings", 19 June 2017), accessed 31.07.2018, http://www.consilium.europa.eu/media/23991/st10387en17-conclusions-on-the-eu-strategy-for-central-asia.pdf, archived at <http://archive.is/IWd9W.

203 Delegation of the European Union to Georgia, "European Commission Vice-President Maroš Šefčovič Highlights Successful EU-Georgia Cooperation in Batumi conference", 14 July 2017, accessed 31.07.2018, http://eeas.europa.eu/delegations/georgia/30039/european-commission-vice-president-maroš-šefčovič-highlights-successful-eu-georgia-cooperation_en, archived at http://archive.is/c2MCo.

204 "Azerbaidzhan i Turkmenistan rasshiriat sotrudnichestvo v oblasti postavok energoresursov v Evropy – Deklaratsiia", *Interfax-Azerbaijan,* 9 August 2017, accessed 31.07.2018, http://interfax.az/view/710267>, archived at <http://archive.is/N3hG5.

205 Maros Sefcovic, "Azerbaijan is a Strategic Energy Partner for EU", *APA,* 18 December 2017, accessed 31.07.2018, http://en.apa.az/azerbaijan-politics/foreign-news/maros-sefcovic-azerbaijan-is-a-strategic-energy-partner-for-eu-interview.htm>, archived at <http://archive.is/gWB7W.

206 Innovation and Networks Executive Agency, European Commission, "Pre-FEED, Reconnaissance Surveys and Strategic and Economic Evaluations of the Trans-Caspian Pipeline", accessed 31.07.2018, http://ec.europa.eu/inea/en/connecting-europe-facility/cef-energy/7.1.1-0007-elaz-s-m-17.

After more than twenty years of negotiation, the five-party Convention on the Status of the Caspian Sea was signed in Aktau, Kazakhstan, on 12 August 2018. Iran had consistently refused to accept less than 20 percent of the Caspian seabed, although by each of the three possible methods of delimitation according to international law, it was only entitled to 13–14 percent. However, the text of the Caspian Convention makes clear that the delimitation will be made according to these generally recognised principles, and that Iran must settle of less than 20 percent. Moreover, the pairs of countries Azerbaijan/Russia, Azerbaijan/Kazakhstan, Kazakhstan/Russia, and Kazakhstan/Turkmenistan (as well as Azerbaijan/Kazakhstan/Russia trilaterally) have for some time agreed to use the "modified median line" method. This allows for joint development of oil and gas deposits near the boundary between them. Indeed, Kazakhstan and Russia implemented this solution in detail some time ago.

The "modified median line" method creates the possibility of adjusting the conditions of the boundaries between contiguous national subsea sectors. Thus, while the Azerbaijan/Iran boundary will likely be where it should be, the two countries have recently finalised an agreement that Iran can participate in developing a deposit in the Azerbaijani sector. This deposit is not named, but it is almost certainly the Alov deposit, where Iran (which calls it Alborz) militarily threatened vessels chartered by BP in 2001, in order to halt development. Likewise, there have been "side deals" made between Turkmenistan and Iran; and Russia has agreed to assist in the development of the offshore Iranian sector. All these promises have convinced Tehran to sign.

For years, Russia and Iran teamed up to make it obligatory that any pipelines on the seabed could be laid only with the consent of all five littoral states. This insistence was aimed at halting the TCGP. For Russia, however, in recent years, blocking that pipeline gradually became less important, while the need to set into order a general security regime became more important. Iran was left isolated. Such unanimity is not required in the convention. Its signed text says plainly that all littoral countries have the right to lay pipelines and cables on the seabed in their national sectors. The subsea sectors of Turkmenistan and Azerbaijan have a border in the centre of the Caspian Sea, so they do not need any other country's permission. This is what they have long insisted, and it is in conformance with general principles of international law. Azerbaijan and Turkmenistan always had the right to build the pipeline, but the signature of the convention clarifies the business environment, providing certainty that is necessary for investment.

In this connection, it is worthwhile noting that a joint study by the World Bank and the European Union about the ecological and environmental impact of the TCGP gave the pipeline a green light several years ago. This puts the pipeline also into conformance with the conditions of the so-called Tehran Convention (Framework Convention for the Protection of the Marine Environment of the Caspian Sea), signed in 2003 and which entered into force 2006. It is no coincidence that the Aktau Protocol to the Tehran Convention, on combating pollution incidents from oil installations, entered into force in July 2016, as the Caspian Convention itself was in the final stages of preparation. Moreover, the Moscow Protocol on Environment Impact Assessment in Transboundary Context was signed on 20 July 2018. It provides that the decision on implementation of any project shall be taken by the "Party(ies) under whose jurisdiction the proposed activity ... is planned to be implemented."[207] Therefore, it is impossible for any littoral state to block any project with a simple veto, even in the theoretical case where there are multiple vetoes.

Furthermore, "any dispute between the Contracting Parties concerning the application or interpretation of the provisions of this Protocol shall be settled in accordance with Article 30 of the Convention," which in turn states that "the Contracting Parties will settle [disputes] by consultations, negotiations or by any other peaceful means of their own choice."[208] One may conclude, particularly in light of the best practices based authoritative study by the World Bank and the EU, that the process of decision-making cannot be abused by countries that might have an interest in halting gas pipeline development, and that the final decision on implementation indeed will be made by the initiating country, which the Protocol calls the "Party of Origin."

There is space in the TANAP and TAP pipelines for gas from Turkmenistan. And that gas is literally at Turkmenistan's shore of the Caspian Sea, where the East–West Pipeline (EWP) carries deposits from the southeast of the country, and where it is now capped, awaiting construction of the TCGP, which the European Commission has selected

---

207 "Protocol on Environmental Impact Assessment in a Transboundary Context to the Framework Convention for the Protection of the Marine Environment of the Caspian Sea", Articles 10 and 1(a), accessed 31.07.2018, http://www.tehranconvention.org/IMG/pdf/PROTOCOL_ON _ENVIRONMENTAL_IMPACT_ASSESSMENT_IN_A_TRANSBOUNDARY _CONTEXT_EN.pdf.

208 Ibid., Article 15; and "Framework Convention for the Protection of the Marine Environment of the Caspian Sea", Article 30, accessed 31.07.2018, http://www.tehranconvention.org/spip .php?article4.

as a Project of Common Interest. Not only are all the building blocks now in place, but also the EU's Connecting Europe Facility and the government of Georgia are funding the preliminary engineering and other studies. After costs are specified, the transportation tariffs can be calculated, and then shippers can negotiate sale–purchase agreements with Turkmenistan.

Conclusion: Azerbaijan, Central Eurasian Energy, and the TCGP

Azerbaijan is one of the foundational vertices of the Azerbaijan–Russia–Turkey triangle, which is in turn the energy geoeconomic basis for the earlier Greater Turco-Caucasian HEC, now West Central Eurasian HEC. The foundational basis of the East Central Eurasian HEC is the triangle China–Kazakhstan–Russia, but over the course of the last decade, Turkmenistan has become so tightly integrated there, and with its main gas fields located in the far southeast of the country, that this triangle is effectively, for some purposes, quadrilateral. But it would be a strange quadrilateral, as Russian–Turkmen energy relations are nearly nonexistent. Of the three triangles formed by Turkmenistan with any pair of vertices from the foundational basis, only China–Kazakhstan–Turkmenistan has any real significance. Considering this, it is clear that Azerbaijan's geographic and geoeconomic situation on the energy map makes it the key link for joining up together not just Azerbaijan and Turkmenistan via the TCGP, but moreover the East and West aspects of the Central Eurasian HEC more generally.

TCGP is, and is insufficiently recognised to be, a strategic pipeline, just like BTC was twenty years ago, which established and reinforced the independence of the participating countries and also happened to be very advantageous commercially. The EU has been trying to help with TCGP for some years, but it is mainly interested in the economic benefit. It does not have the political weight that the United States does to declare, as it did for the BTC, that this is a strategic project that will help again to clarify and stabilise the situation in Georgia both economically and politically, as well as to extend in a positive way Western influence onto the eastern shore of the Caspian Sea.

The TCGP is also a demonstration project. Without it, the undersea Kazakhstan–Azerbaijan oil pipeline will be discouraged. Just as the BTC made possible the SCP and SGC, the TCGP will be a signal to international investors and politicians that not only it, but also other projects, may go forward. Such a development in the energy geoeconomics would naturally influence the regional geopolitics, making it possible for Turkmenistan and Kazakhstan to rely politically, not only economically, upon the West in order to balance the various interests that they have to balance, such as encroachments by Russian and especially Chinese influence.

Thus with TCGP realised, and after Kazakhstan's offshore Kashagan deposit ramps up production, we may look forward to the realisation of the Trans-Caspian Oil Transport System (TCOTS), which Azerbaijan and Kazakhstan have been planning for over a decade. The project calls for constructing the 739-kilometre KCTS pipeline overland from Eskene to Kuryk in Kazakhstan, which would open into a 700-kilometre Trans-Caspian Oil Pipeline (TCOP) running from Kuryk, near Aktau port, underneath the sea to Baku.

There has been a long-term plan for this oil from Kazakhstan to transit to Georgia's Black Sea coast, from where tankers would take it the Ukrainian port of Odessa. There, it would enter the planned Euro-Asian Oil Transportation Corridor (EAOTC) via the Odessa–Brody Pipeline (OBP; now sometimes called the Sarmatia pipeline). The OBP, reversed back to its originally intended southeast-to-northwest direction inside Ukraine, is in the process of being extended to Plock, where there is a refinery, with plans then to extend it finally to the port of Gdansk. At least a part of this oil from Aktau could be diverted via Baku to Ceyhan via the BTC pipeline, a version designated as the ABC pipeline (for Aktau–Baku–Ceyhan).[209]

Through connection with Azerbaijan, Turkmenistan will finally find its place in the Euro-Caspian energy complex. Every effort is being made, and should be made, to implement the extension of the SGC to Central Asia, and Turkmenistan in the first instance. In the more distant future, natural gas from Kazakhstan's offshore Kashagan deposit may also be targeted for export to Europe through an undersea pipeline, first conceived a decade ago, landing also in Azerbaijan.

---

209 Robert M. Cutler, "Kazakhstan and Azerbaijan Plan an Undersea Trans-Caspian Oil Pipeline", *Central Asia – Caucasus Analyst,* 7 November 2016, accessed 31.07.2018, http://www.cacianalyst .org/publications/analytical-articles/item/13407-kazakhstan-and-azerbaijan-plan-an-undersea -trans-caspian-oil-pipeline.html.

CHAPTER 5
Azerbaijan and Turkey: Analysis of Mutual Cooperation and Strategic Relations since the Independence of Azerbaijan

Shamkhal Abilov

Introduction

The motto of "one nation, two states" captures the sense of solidarity and friendship between Azerbaijan and Turkey since the dissolution of the Soviet Union in 1991. The close relationship between these two states is not only based on cultural, linguistic, and ethnic characteristics, but also grounded in shared political, economic, and strategic interests. Good bilateral relations and interactions at the official and national level have been almost unique, and reflect the ideological and pragmatic approach of both states. As both sides understand each other easily due to linguistic proximity, it has proved equally simple for the two countries to overcome Azerbaijan's imposed cultural isolation during the seven decades of the Soviet Union and to build societal, economic, and political links with each other.

Relations with Turkey—the first country to recognise the independence of Azerbaijan in 1991—have been an essential precept for the foreign strategy of post-independence Azerbaijan. Thus, since its independence, the country's main foreign policy aims have been to export its energy resources to Western markets, in order to facilitate economic development; to decrease its dependence on Russia; to increase its economic and military power, in order to liberate its occupied territories from Armenia; and to build a secular state.[210] Requiring a reliable partner to help

---

210 Houman Sadri, "Elements of Azerbaijan Foreign Policy", *Journal of Third World Studies*, 20 (1), 2003: 187-188.

achieve its policy objectives, Azerbaijan has considered Turkey as its sole strategic supporter in addressing both domestic and international security and economic problems.[211]

The reasons that led Azerbaijan to choose Turkey as a sole partner were the historical, cultural, and linguistic links and mutual confidence between two states; Turkey's direct border connection with the Mediterranean Sea and Europe; and Turkey's existing alliances with Western countries.[212] Thus, Turkey was recognised as an important link for Azerbaijan to gain access to international and European markets and to integrate into the Euro-Atlantic space. In order to show the significance of Turkey's role in the foreign policy of Azerbaijan, Tofig Gasimov, the former Minister of Foreign Affairs, commented during his visit to Ankara in August 1992 that, "Turkey is our greatest helper. We want Turkey's aid in establishing links with the world."[213]

With regard to Turkey's geopolitical interests in Azerbaijan after the dissolution of the Soviet Union, it should be noted that for decades, Turkey had built its foreign policy in the context of its geopolitical proximity with the Soviet Union. This location made it the sole regional partner for the Western Bloc during the Cold War. However, with the collapse of the Soviet Union and end of the Cold War, Turkey's geopolitical importance also disappeared. Moreover, the rejection of Turkey's application for membership of the European Community in 1989 pushed the country to look for a new geopolitical role, in order to preserve its regional power status. Therefore, building its influence over the newly independent states of Eurasia after the demise of the Soviet Union was an opportunity for Turkey to regain the strategic significance it had enjoyed during the Cold War period.[214]

The dissolution of the Soviet Union raised hopes in Turkey for the "unification" of all Turkish populations of this region. It was anticipated that this would further increase the country's importance as a bridge between Europe and Asia, and extend its role as a leader and model

---

211 Mehmet Dikkaya and Jason E. Strakes, "A Paradigm Shift in Turkish-Azerbaijani Relations? Result for Turkish Armenian Reconciliation Process between 2008 and 2010", *Review of Socio-Economic Perspectives*, 2 (1), 2017: 90-91.

212 Cavid Valiyev, "Azərbaycan-Türkiyə münasibətləri: 1991-2016", in *Azərbaycan Respublikasının xarici siyasətinin əsas istiqamətləri (1991-2016)*, ed. Fərhad Məmmədov, Cavid Vəliyev, and Aqşin Məmmədov "Poliart" MMC, 2017, 103.

213 Kursat Cinar, "Turkey and Turkic Nations: A Post-Cold War Analysis of Relations", *Turkish Studies*, 14 (2), 2013: 264.

214 Svante E. Cornell, *Azerbaijan since Independence*, New York: M. E. Sharpe, 2011, 365.

secular state, not only in this part of Eurasia but throughout the Islamic world. Turkey's optimism in this respect was illustrated in the inauguration speech of President Turgut Ozal to the Turkish Grand National Assembly in 1989, where he stated: "The end of the Cold War and the dissolution of the USSR provided Turkey with a historical opportunity to be leader of the region ... Turkey should have not missed such an opportunity that appeared first time after 400 years."[215] Turkey was also seeking economic benefits from the post-Soviet countries, by playing a leading role in the transportation of their huge hydrocarbon resources to the West.[216] Due to its geographical proximity with other Turkic states that possess vast hydrocarbon resources, and its historical and cultural links with Turkey, Azerbaijan presented a unique political and strategic opportunity in the formulation of Turkey's policy towards the Turkic states of the former Soviet Union. International relations scholar Suha Bolukbasi has outlined Turkey's long-term policy towards Azerbaijan as follows: support for Azerbaijan's independence; support for Azerbaijani sovereignty over Karabakh; prevention or restriction of Russian presence and influence in the region; participation in Azerbaijani oil production and export; and the maintenance of a friendly (but not necessarily pan-Turkic) Azerbaijani administration.[217]

This study intends to examine the political and strategic relations between Azerbaijan and Turkey since the beginning of 1990s, and to analyse the reasons that both states have adopted friendly relations from geopolitical and strategic perspectives. In addition, the complexity of Turkey's stance towards the Nagorno-Karabakh conflict will be investigated, including Turkey's efforts to find a solution to the conflict within the framework of respecting the territorial integrity of Azerbaijan and to preserve the position of Azerbaijan at an international level; the rapprochement between Turkey and Armenia within the Caucasus Stability and Cooperation Platform of Turkey; and its political and strategic impact over the relations between Azerbaijan and Turkey. Besides political and strategic relations, economic relations between two states,

215 Lutfu Sagbansua and Nurettin Can, "Shanghai Cooperation Organization, Turkic Republics and Turkey: Economic and Business Dimensions", *Canadian Social Science*, 7 (2), 2011: 82.
216 Freddy De Pauw, "Turkey's Policies in Transcaucasia", in *Contested Borders in the Caucasus*, ed. Bruno Coppieters, Brussell: VUB Press, 1996.
217 Suha Bolukbasi, "Ankara's Baku-Centered Transcaucasia Policy: Has It Failed?", *Middle East Journal*, 51 (1), 1997: 80.

particularly in regard to cooperation on hydrocarbon resources, will also be covered by this study.

Azerbaijani-Turkish Relations between 1991-2008

From Euphoria to Pragmatism

As mentioned before, Turkey was the first country that recognised the independence of Azerbaijan on 9 November 1991, almost one month before it recognised the independence of other former Soviet countries. Turkey subsequently upgraded its consulate in Baku to the embassy level in January 1992. At that time, Azerbaijan's president was Ayaz Mutalli-bov, the country's former Communist Party leader, who was well known for favouring a pro-Russian foreign policy.[218] The suspicious behaviour of Mutallibov, pertaining to the full independence of Azerbaijan that was declared on 18 October 1991, should be noted. His conflicting alle-giances became clear in his November speech to parliament, in which he attempted to justify Gorbachev's New Union plan by arguing that "Moscow has abolished more than 80 central government ministries, the-re is no structure to dictate to us like before. The Centre will only take care of foreign and security policy, which too will be coordinated with us."[219] Consequently, when the Soviet Union collapsed and the presi-dents of Russia, Ukraine, and Belarus established the Commonwealth of Independent States (CIS) on 8 December 1991, Mutallibov acted as if Azerbaijan was already a member and signed the Alma-Ata Protocol to join the organisation on 21 December.[220] Thus, due to the pro-Russian policy of Mutallibov, Azerbaijan was not able to build close relations with Turkey until the following summer.

When Abulfez Elchibey became president of Azerbaijan in June 1992, relations between Azerbaijan and Turkey skyrocketed due to the person-al efforts of the presidents of both countries. The main foreign policy priority of the Elchibey government was to dissociate Azerbaijan from Russia's post-Soviet activities and instead to develop high-level relations

---

218 Ibid., 83.
219 Shamkhal Abilov and Ismayil Isayev, "Azerbaijan-Russian Relations: Azerbaijan's Pursuit of Successful Balanced Foreign Policy", *Journal of Central Asian & Caucasian Studies*, 9 (19), 2015: 119.
220 Ibid., 119.

with Turkey and Western countries,[221] including support for the expansion of Turkish influence in Azerbaijan. Turgut Ozal, Turkey's president, meanwhile acted as an advocate of Azerbaijan in the international arena until his death in 1993,[222] recognising Azerbaijan as a gateway to the other Turkic states of Central Asia. During the first summit of Turkish-speaking heads of state in Ankara in October 1992, Ozal proclaimed the twenty-first century as the age of the Turks. He also recommended the formation of a Turkish common market and Turkish Development and Investment Bank, proposals which were welcomed only by Elchibey.[223] During the period of Elchibey, these friendly relations ensured the position of Turkey towards Azerbaijan was more realistic. During that time, Turkish businessmen came to Baku to research the Azerbaijani economy, with business more easily conducted than in other countries due to the cultural and linguistic proximity between the two states ; while Turkish music, television programmes, and soap operas became famous in Azerbaijan.[224] According to Michael Croissant, there were three main factors that drove Azerbaijan to pursue a pro-Turkish policy during the Elchibey period:

- The Popular Front of Azerbaijan (PFA), and Elchibey in particular, held ardently pro-Turkish (and in some respects pan-Turkic) views, believing that Azerbaijan's ethno-linguistic heritage made Turkey a natural choice as Baku's main external partner.
- Turkey represented the model of a secular, democratic, market-oriented state to which Azerbaijan could aspire.
- Turkey—through its ties with NATO and the West—offered Azerbaijan a potential means through which to offset Russia's perceived bias in favour of Armenia in the Nagorno-Karabakh struggle.[225]

However, Azerbaijani–Turkish relations changed following the replacement of Elchibey with Heydar Aliyev in 1993. A pragmatic leader, Aliyev understood the benefit of following a balanced foreign policy towards regional powers, such as Iran and Russia, in order to

221 Ibid., 121.
222 Dikkaya and Strakes, "A Paradigm Shift in Turkish-Azerbaijani Relations?", 85.
223 Cagla Gul Yesevi and Burcu Yavus Tiftikcigil, "Turkey-Azerbaijan Energy Relations: A Political and Economic Analysis", *International Journal of Energy Economics and Policy*, 5 (1), 2015: 28.
224 Fariz Ismailzade, "Turkey-Azerbaijan: The Honeymoon is Over", *Turkish Policy Quarterly*, 4 (4), 2005: 3.
225 Michael P. Croissant, *The Armenia-Azerbaijan Conflict: Causes and Implications,* Westport: Praeger Publisher, 1998, 82.

consolidate Azerbaijan's independence. Accordingly, he reconsidered the strict pro-Turkish policy of the Elchibey government, annulled treaties between Azerbaijan and Turkey signed during the previous administration, set a visa regime by which Turkish citizens could enter Azerbaijan, and dismissed 1,600 Turkish military experts who were training Azerbaijani forces.[226] Meanwhile, Azerbaijan joined as a member the Commonwealth of Independence States (CIS), the regional organisation created by Russia in order to preserve its influence over the former Soviet states, and restored the relations with its northern neighbour.[227] These acts were viewed by some Turkish politicians as a victory for Russia, leading the Turkish ambassador to Baku to be linked to Rovshan Javadov, who led an unsuccessful coup d'état against Aliyev in 1995.

When the Welfare Party, an Islamist political party that changed the policy direction of Turkey towards the Middle East, came to power in 1995, relations became even worse. At that time, partly due to the coup scandal and partly political affairs inside Turkey, it proved difficult to establish warm relations between the two countries. It was only after the Welfare Party left power that Azerbaijan and Turkey restored warm relations and began to develop friendly and strategic ties. From that point on, both countries have tried hard to maintain friendly relations, as many consider that "Turkish-Azerbaijani relations were more important than relations between two ordinary states. It was more like a relation between two brothers."[228] Both states understand that they need each other in order to pursue their foreign policy goals, especially in terms of the energy issue. For transporting its energy resources to European markets while bypassing Russia, Baku requires strategic cooperation from Ankara. Meanwhile, Turkey needs Azerbaijan as a gateway to the Central Asia, as well as to decrease its energy dependence on Russia and to transform itself into an energy hub for transporting hydrocarbon resources from the region to Europe. Cooperation on energy issues and partnership in transport routes for oil became the cornerstones of relations between Azerbaijan and Turkey in the last decades of the twentieth century. At the OSCE Istanbul Summit in 1999, the countries joined Georgia, Kazakhstan, and the United States in signing the Baku–Tbilisi–Ceyhan (BTC) Declaration. By this act, both parties were bound to each other not only

---

226 Svante E. Cornell, "Turkey and the Conflict in Nagorno Karabakh: A Delicate Balance", *Middle Eastern Studies*, 34 (1), 1998: 62.

227 Ismailzade, "Turkey-Azerbaijan", 4.

228 Ibid., 4.

through common geopolitical interests, but also economically.[229] However, despite all the ups and downs, if one looks at the general picture at
that time, it is possible to say that the position of Turkey regarding to the
Nagorno-Karabakh conflict and its diplomatic support for Azerbaijan at
the international level shaped relations between the two states during the
first decade of Azerbaijan's independence.

The Position of Turkey in the Nagorno-Karabakh Conflict

From the outset of the Nagorno-Karabakh conflict, Turkey tried to present itself as a natural mediator helping the belligerents to resolve the
dispute peacefully. However, Turkey's intention to remain impartial did
not last long.[230] Following the massacre of the civilian population in the
Azerbaijani town of Khojaly on the night of 26 February 1992,[231] Turkish policy towards the conflict changed dramatically. In response to the
massacre, large demonstrations were organised in Turkey, with hundreds
of thousands of protestors in favor of Turkish military intervention in
support of Azerbaijan.

Due to strong pro-Azerbaijani public opinion, it was impossible for
the Turkish government to preserve its neutral position and increasingly
hard for it to disregard public demands.[232] Therefore, President Turgut
Ozal publicly warned the Armenian side on several occasions that it was
responsible for the results of its aggression in the territory of Azerbaijan,
while adding that Armenia should be "a little frightened." This shocked
Armenians and the Armenian diaspora throughout the world, and "enabled the latter especially to pursue a policy of discrediting Turkey as
planning a 'new' genocide on Armenians."[233] While condemning the dual
policy of world powers towards the Nagorno-Karabakh conflict, Turgut
Ozal stated during his speech at the Turkish Grant National Assembly
on 17 February 1992: "If Western countries support Armenia, which does

---

229 Ibid., 5.
230 Svante E. Cornell, *Small Nations and Great Powers: A Study of Ethnopolitical Conflict in the Cauca-
     sus,* London: Routledge Curzon, 2001, 284.
231 Shamkhal Abilov and Ismayil Isayev, "The Consequences of the Nagorno-Karabakh War for
     Azerbaijan and the Undeniable Reality of Khojaly Massacre: A View from Azerbaijan", *Polish
     Political Science Yearbook,* 45, 2016: 295-296.
232 Scott A. Jones, "Turkish Strategic Interest in the Transcaucasus", in *Crossroads and Conflict:
     Security and Foreign Policy in the Caucasus and Central Asia,* ed. Gary K. Bertsch et al., London:
     Routledge, 2000, 61-62.
233 Cornell, *Small Nations and Great Powers,* 284.

not accept any peace talks or negotiations, therefore, a regional war will be inevitable between both parties."[234] Due to these developments, at the beginning of March, Turkey announced the inspection of all flights to Armenia that passed over Turkish airspace.[235]

Tensions between Turkey and Armenia flared in May 1992 when Armenian military troops occupied Shusha.[236] As a result, Turkey began military exercises near the border with Armenia, which Russia considered to be a direct threat. Therefore, Marshall Yevgeny Shaposhnikov, the supreme commander of the CIS, stated: "We are carefully watching Turkey's activities in the Caucasus."[237] Following the fall of Lachin to Armenian forces on 17 May 1992, the fighting between the countries spread to Nakhichevan, an autonomous region of Azerbaijan, which increased tensions between Turkey and Armenia. When Heydar Aliyev, the speaker of Nakhichevan, called on Turkey for help, President Turgut Ozal stated that, without any hesitation, Turkey would send troops to Nakhichevan.[238] General Chief of Staff of the Turkish Armed Forces, Dogan Gures, added that "he was prepared to send to the Karabakh conflict as many soldiers as the government of Azerbaijan requested."[239] In light of this development, Russian Defence Minister Pavel Grachev together with Gennady Burbulis, the right-hand man of Russian President Boris Yeltsin, travelled to Armenia in May 1992 to face down the Turkish military threat.[240] Grachev stated that "Russia has its own interests in Azerbaijan [and] we will not permit interference by Turkish troops."[241] Marshal Shaposhnikov also appealed to NATO, stating that "Turkey's intervention could create a Third World War."[242] However, unlike President Turgut Ozal, Suleyman Demirel, the Prime Minister

---

234 Suleyman Elik, *Iran-Turkey Relations 1979-2011: Conceptualizing the Dynamics of Politics, Religion and Security in the Middle-Power States,* London: Routledge, 2012, 109.
235 Cornell, "Turkey and the Conflict in Nagorno Karabakh", 61.
236 Ceyhun Mahmudlu and Shamkhal Abilov, "The Peace-making Process in the Nagorno-Karabakh Conflict: Why Did Iran Fail in its Mediation Effort?", *Journal of Contemporary Central and Eastern Europe*, 2017: 2.
237 Elik, *Iran-Turkey Relations 1979-2011,* 109.
238 Garey Goldberg, "Moscow Sees War Threat if Outsiders Act in Karabakh", *Los Angeles Times*, 21 May 1992, accessed 20.05.2018, http://articles.latimes.com/1992-05-21/news/mn -337_1_karabakh-conflict.
239 Pauw, "Turkey's Policies in Transcaucasia".
240 Thomas De Wall, *Black Garden: Armenia and Azerbaijan through Peace and War,* New York: New York University Press, 2003, 203.
241 Pauw, "Turkey's Policies in Transcaucasia".
242 Bahruz Balayev, *The Right to Self-determination in the South Caucasus: Nagorno Karabakh in Context,* Lanham: Lexington Books, 2013, 71.

of Turkey, was less outspoken about the Turkish military intervention. Demirel believed that a military intervention by Turkey would be a political mistake,[243] confirming that "I will never do that unless getting the support of great powers behind Turkey."[244]

Generally speaking, despite the fundamental differences between the two countries, the Turkish government had tried to preserve its moderate position towards Armenia in order to save bilateral relations. Turkey was the second country that recognised the independence of Armenia in 1991, and it also reopened the historical railway between Kars and Gyumri, which was followed by unofficial links between the two governments for the creation of diplomatic relations and official border agreements.[245] Later on, the Turkish government refused to establish full diplomatic relations with Armenia, partly due to its aggression against Azerbaijan and partly because Paragraph 11 of the Armenian Declaration of Independence—adopted by the Armenian Supreme Council on 23 August 1990—stated that "the Republic of Armenia supports international recognition of the 1915 Armenian genocide in Ottoman Turkey and Western Armenia."[246] However, the governments on both sides tried to establish positive relations without full diplomatic recognition. In 1992, Hikmet Chetin, the foreign minister of Turkey, declared that his country was ready for the development of the diplomatic relations if Armenian forces withdrew from Shusha and Lachin. The Turkish government also agreed to sell 100,000 tons of grain to Armenia in September 1992, and signed a deal to supply Armenia with 300 million kilowatts of electricity annually while it was suffering from energy shortages.[247]

The agreement on selling electricity to Armenia was not acceptable to the government of Azerbaijan, because it would undermine the energy blockade which was Baku's main means of political leverage. Azerbaijan took the position towards Turkey that "they claim to be our brothers, but give bread to our enemies."[248] Tofig Gasimov, the foreign minister of Azerbaijan, called the energy deal between Armenia and Turkey

243 Goldberg, "Moscow Sees War Threat if Outsiders Act in Karabakh".
244 Shamkhal Abilov, "The Discourse 'One Nation Two State': The Position of Turkey in the Nagorno-Karabakh Conflict", *Journal of Caspian Affairs*, 1 (2), 2015: 34.
245 Fiona Hill et al., "Armenia and Turkey: From Normalization to Reconciliation", *Turkish Policy Quarterly*, 13 (4), 2015: 132-133.
246 Rovshan Ibrahimov, "Turkish-Azerbaijani Relations and Turkey's Policy in the Central Asia", *The Caucasus & Globalization: Journal of Social, Political and Economic Studies*, 5 (3-4), 2011: 17.
247 Bolukbasi, "Ankara's Baku-Centered Transcaucasia Policy", 84-85.
248 Cornell, "Turkey and the Conflict in Nagorno Karabakh", 67.

a stab in the back to Azerbaijan. Therefore, due to the strong reaction and criticism from Azerbaijan and the main opposition party in Turkey, Demirel's government suspended the deal without implementation in November 1992.[249] Furthermore, the intensification of the Nagorno-Karabakh conflict—with significant military attacks by Armenia at the end of March 1993 and the occupation of the Kalbajar district of Azerbaijan on 3 April 1993—worsened relations between the two countries and placed Ankara in a difficult position. As a result, Turkey decided to close its land border with Armenia and to join Azerbaijan in an economic embargo against its rival.[250]

The summer of 1993 witnessed political disorder in the capital of Azerbaijan.[251] Armenians used this turmoil as an opportunity to occupy other Azerbaijani territories in the east and southeast parts of Nagorno-Karabakh, which carried the conflict again into Nakhichevan. As a result, Turkey threatened Armenia with military intervention and began to deploy military units along its border with Armenia in September 1993, in order to show its intent in the event of an invasion of Nakhichevan.[252] Statements by the Turkish political and military leadership significantly increased concerns on the Armenian side. Therefore, Armenia requested that Russia deploy its forces to the Turkey–Armenia border, in order to avoid a direct military threat by Turkey. Russia again backed Armenia in the Nakhichevan case and moved its troops to the border, showing its willingness to confront Turkey in the event of military intervention against Armenia.[253]

Generally speaking, even though Turkey showcased a pro-Azerbaijan position throughout 1992 and 1993, the country failed to provide tangible support to Baku in the Nagorno-Karabakh War.[254] Therefore, it is worth considering why Ankara chose not to intervene in the conflict. Scholars have identified various internal and external factors that affected Turkish policy on the war, particularly in its early stages. These include the doctrine of Kemalism, the scope of differing opinions among the political

249 Bolukbasi, "Ankara's Baku-Centered Transcaucasia Policy", 85.
250 Aybars Görgülü, *Turkey-Armenian Relations: A Vicious Circle,* TESEV Publications, 2008, 11-12.
251 Abilov and Isayev, "Azerbaijan-Russian Relations", 123.
252 Alec Rasizade, "Azerbaijan's Prospects in Nagorno-Karabakh", *Mediterranean Quarterly*, 22 (3), 2011, 82.
253 Dmitrii Trenin, *Russia's Use of Military Forces in Intra-State Conflicts in the CIS*, Bundesinstitut fur Ostwissenschaftliche und Internationale Studien, 1996, 2009-2014.
254 Umut Uzer, "Nagorno-Karabakh in Regional and World Politics: A Case Study for Nationalism, Realism and Ethnic Conflict", *Journal of Muslim Minority Affairs*, 32 (2), 2012: 249.

leadership, Turkey's relations with the West, the existence of Russia as a regional power, the so-called Armenian Genocide, Turkey's domestic security in the early 1990s, and the reputation of Turkey in the West in respect to the Cyprus issue of 1974.[255] It should also be added that there was never an official request from Azerbaijan for Turkish military intervention in the Nagorno-Karabakh conflict.[256] Nonetheless, all these factors did not prevent Turkey from giving diplomatic support to Azerbaijan and engaging in various diplomatic initiatives, in order to elucidate and justify Azerbaijan's stand in the conflict at the regional and international level.

Turkey made a concerted effort to bring the case to the agenda of the Conference on Security and Cooperation in Europe, and was the main initiator of a meeting of the organisation in Prague on 28 February 1992, where the member countries confirmed the territorial integrity of Azerbaijan.[257] In 1991 and 1992, Turkish diplomats conducted various rounds of shuttle diplomacy, not only between the parties in the conflict, but also in European countries. In addition, Hikmet Chetin used Turkey's connections to the West to draw the attention of the governments of Western states. He even personally raised the issue of the Nagorno-Karabakh conflict in a phone call to James Baker, Secretary of State of the United States.[258] Moreover, Ankara also raised the issue in the UN Security Council, alerting the five permanent members of the organisation to Armenian aggression.[259]

In 1992, Turkey initiated a peace proposal, based on a "territorial swap" plan developed by Paul Goble, special adviser to James Baker. According to the proposal, the territory of Armenia that connected Azerbaijan with Nakhichevan should be entrusted to Azerbaijan. In return, Azerbaijan should assign part of Nagorno-Karabakh to Armenia. As a result, Azerbaijan would have direct land connection with Nakhichevan and Armenia with Nagorno-Karabakh.[260] However, neither party welcomed this plan. In the summer of 1992, at the Rome session of the Organisation for Security and Cooperation in Europe, the Minsk Group was established with the aim of managing official negotiations to find

---

255 Cornell, *Azerbaijan since Independence*, 369-371.
256 Abilov, "The Discourse 'One Nation Two State'", 37-38.
257 Bolukbasi, "Ankara's Baku-Centered Transcaucasia Policy", 84.
258 Cornell, *Small Nations and Great Powers*, 368.
259 Pauw, "Turkey's Policies in Transcaucasia".
260 Paul A. Goble, "Coping with the Nagorno-Karabakh Crisis", *The Fletcher Forum*, 16 (2), 1992: 26.

a solution to the conflict.[261] However, this initiative failed because of disagreements between the parties. After six months, Russia, the United States, and Turkey met for private discussions about the conflict resolution, later known as the "3+1 initiative." The inaugural stage of the proposal called on the parties to maintain a sixty-day ceasefire, as groundwork for a two-level negotiation process.[262] In accordance with this agreement, Armenian military forces would withdraw from Kalbajar, an occupied region of Azerbaijan, within two months. During this time, new peace negotiations would begin. Although at first both sides accepted the proposal, Armenia raised concerns regarding the position of Karabakh Armenians. As a result, this group refused the "3+1 initiative" in May 1993, arguing that there were not enough "guarantees for the Karabakh Armenians and the proposal's exclusion of the elimination of the embargo put on Karabakh by Azerbaijan."[263]

After the occupation of Kalbajar on 3 April 1993, Turkey together with Pakistan succeeded in orchestrating an adaptation of Resolution 822 of the United Nation Security Council on 30 April.[264] That May, Turkey initiated another peace plan, together with Russia and the United States. Proposed in July and labelled "a diplomatic attack" by the Turkish press, the plan involved "telephone diplomacy" between US President Bill Clinton, President Boris Yeltsin of Russia, and French President François Mitterrand, and summoned representatives of Sweden, then chair of the CSCE, and Italy, chair of the Minsk Group.[265] Meanwhile, a further proposal called for the deployment to Azerbaijan of United Nations peacekeepers, including forces from Turkey. However, this was perceived by Armenia and Russia as Turkish military intervention, causing Russia to reject the proposal.[266] On 17 August 1993, Turkey appealed to the UN Security Council, regarding to the Armenian attack on Fizuli and the Jebrail region of Azerbaijan. A day later, the Security Council issued a declaration that demanded the withdrawal of Armenian military

261 Shamkhal Abilov, "OSCE Minsk Group: Proposals and Failure, the View from Azerbaijan", *Insight Turkey*, 20 (1), 2018: 143.
262 Wendy Betts, "Third Party Mediation: An Obstacle to Peace in Nagorno Karabakh", *SAIS Review*, 19 (2), 1999: 169.
263 Bahar Başer, "Third Party Mediation in Nagorno-Karabakh: Part of the Cure or Part of the Disease?", *Journal of Central Asian & Caucasian Studies*, 3 (5), 2008: 92.
264 Abilov, "The Discourse 'One Nation Two State'", 41.
265 Pauw, "Turkey's Policies in Transcaucasia".
266 Stephen J. Blank et al., *Turkey's Strategic Position at the Crossroads of World Affairs* (University Press of the Pacific, 1993), 63.

forces from the recently-occupied territories of Azerbaijan immediately and without any precondition.[267]

Along with the support in international diplomatic and political circles, during those years, Turkey also provided continuous military support to the Azerbaijani army. Moreover, Turkey assisted in solving the refugee and IDP crisis in Azerbaijan during the early 1990s, helping with humanitarian aid, establishing Turkish camps,[268] enforcing Azerbaijan's economic embargo on Armenia, preventing humanitarian aid to Armenia from Western countries from passing through its territory, and refusing to normalise relations with Armenia until it withdrew from occupied territory in Azerbaijan.

Turkey maintained its position regarding the Nagorno-Karabakh conflict after the ceasefire agreement between Azerbaijan and Armenia in May 1994.[269] In all meetings of the OSCE Minsk Group, it strongly supported the position of Azerbaijan. Turkey was also effective in supporting intense lobbying in favour of a declaration on the territorial integrity of Azerbaijan during the Lisbon Summit,[270] which resulted in the acceptance of the Lisbon Principles at the OSCE Summit on 2–3 December 1996.[271] In those years, various agreements and protocols were also signed between Azerbaijan and Turkey in the fields of military, defence, security, naval, and border control.[272]

Ups and Downs between Azerbaijan and Turkey in the First Decade of the Twenty-First Century

Strong cooperation between the brotherly nations of Azerbaijan and Turkey has also extended to the economic, cultural, and social fields. However, at the beginning of this century, it has witnessed some setbacks which have made clear the need for both parties to act with great

---

267 Pauw, "Turkey's Policies in Transcaucasia".

268 Ismailzade, "Turkey-Azerbaijan", 6.

269 Ceyhun Mahmudlu and Agil Ahmadov, "High Degree Autonomous Status for Nagorno Karabakh and Its Possible Role in the Solution of the Conflict," *Journal of Qafqaz University-History, Law and Political Science*, 2 (2), 2014: 115.

270 Svante Cornell, "Turkey's Role and Prospects in the Nagorno-Karabakh Conflict and Its Regional Implications", *Marco Polo Magazine*, 1 (4-5), 1998: 19-23.

271 "Statement of the OSCE Chairman-in-Office", *Annex 1 to the Declaration of the OSCE Lisbon Summit 3 December*, 1996: 15.

272 Mehmet Fatih Öztarsu, "Military Relations of Turkey and Azerbaijan", *Strategic Outlook*, 1 (2), 2011: 2-3-4.

responsibility in preserving high-level cooperation. There were various reasons for these setbacks. The first was the replacement of Turkish President Suleyman Demirel by Ahmet Necdet Sezer in 2000. Unlike Demirel, who was a professional politician and paid attention to the long-term interests of the country, Sezer was a lawyer and aimed to build bilateral relations with neighbouring countries based on the rule of law and democracy. Thus, in comparison to the strong partnership and bilateral relations between two states in 1990s, Turkey faced difficulties in maintaining warm and friendly relations with the government of Azerbaijan during Sezer's presidential term.[273]

The second and most influential factor that led to a setback was the election of the Justice and Development Party, an Islamist party, to the government of Turkey in late 2002. Thus, Turkey's interest in the Caucasus began to decline as the new Turkish government turned West, looking to increase its ties with the European Union and achieve regional leadership in the Middle East. Turkish foreign policy priorities in Azerbaijan were limited to the realisation of the energy projects that had been established from the mid-1990s. This ambition was linked mainly to Turkey's aim to establish itself as an energy hub between East and West, buying energy at low prices from energy-producing countries of the former Soviet Union and selling it to the European market at high prices.[274] As a result, bilateral relations based on pragmatism rather than ideology, and above all on economic interests in the energy field, began to develop between Azerbaijan and Turkey, serving the national interests of both states. Consequently, the implementation of energy deals and energy transportation projects became the main development focus and the cornerstone of relations between the two states.

After long and intense negotiations, the construction of the Baku–Tbilisi–Ceyhan (BTC) oil pipeline and Baku–Tbilisi–Erzurum (BTE) gas pipeline, put into operation in 2005 and 2007 respectively, had great strategic importance in terms of bilateral relations between Azerbaijan and Turkey, and in the realisation of their ambition to transport energy resources to the European market. The parties also agreed to construct two more pipelines, the Trans Adriatic Pipeline (TAP) and Trans Anatolian Natural Gas Pipeline (TANAP), as a continuation of BTE, in order

273 Ismailzade, "Turkey-Azerbaijan", 6.
274 Svante E. Cornell, "Turkey's Role: Balancing the Armenia-Azerbaijan Conflict and Turkish-Armenian Relations", in *The International Politics of the Armenian-Azerbaijani Conflict: The Original "Frozen Conflict" and European Security*, ed. Svante E. Cornell, Palgrave Macmillan, 2017, 91-94.

to transport natural gas from the Caspian Sea to the European market. This will decrease dependence of the European countries on Russia and increase the strategic importance of Azerbaijan as an energy-producing country and Turkey as an energy-transporting country.[275] Thus, while analysing the factors that set back relations between two states, it is possible to say that these paved the way for the replacement of ideological pan-Turkic solidarity of the 1990s with rational and calculated relations based on pragmatism. It should also be mentioned that, in light of these setbacks, there were divergent opinions and an increasing number of negative voices regarding the Nagorno-Karabakh conflict and Turkey's position in this issue.[276]

Meanwhile, there has been an increasing tendency since that time to base relations between Turkey and Armenia on the "zero problems" foreign policy of the Turkish government, which seeks to maintain good neighbourly cooperation with bordering countries in a broader perspective. This tendency has been reflected in the restoration of the Akhtamar Church in Van, the mass demonstrations after the assassination of Armenian editor and journalist Hrant Dink in Turkey, the membership accession process of Turkey to the European Union that began to take new momentum in 2004, and finally the processes that began with the visit of Turkish President Abdullah Gul to Armenia in September 2008, to watch a football match between the two national football teams. The Five-Day War between Georgia and Russia in August 2008 also had a significant impact on bilateral relations between Turkey and Armenia, which had been suspended since 1993 due to the Nagorno-Karabakh conflict.[277]

275 Bayram Balci, "Strengths and Constraints of Turkish Policy in the South Caucasus", *Insight Turkey*, 16 (2), 2014: 44.
276 Cavid Vəliyev, "Regional hadisələrin Türkiyə-Azərbaycan münasibətlərinə təsiri", in *Azərbaycan-Türkiyə əlaqələri son 20 ildə: uğurlar və imkanlar*, ed. Cavid Vəliyev et al., Bakı, 2011, 21.
277 Aybars Görgülü, "Toward a Turkish-Armenian Rapprochement?", *Insight Turkey*, 11 (2), 2009: 19-24.

Azerbaijani-Turkish Relations after 2008: The Implications of Development after 2008 on the Foreign Policy of Azerbaijan

Turkish-Armenian Rapprochement and its Impact on Relations between Azerbaijan and Turkey

The developments in South Caucasus in the summer of 2008 changed the geopolitical situation in the whole region. The Five-Day War between Russia and Georgia, lasting from 7 to 11 August, ended with a Russian military victory and Russia's acknowledgement of the independence and sovereignty of Abkhazia and South Ossetia.[278] In light of these developments, Turkey proposed the establishment of the Caucasus Stability and Cooperation Platform (CSCP). After several rounds of shuttle diplomacy between Georgia, Azerbaijan, and Russia, on 13 August, the Turkish Prime Minister Recep Tayyip Erdoğan introduced a multilateral diplomatic initiative for promoting peace, stability, and cooperation among the countries of the South Caucasus, including Turkey and Russia. This new Turkish foreign policy is based on the "zero problems" concept, intended to establish multilateral relations and achieve maximum cooperation with neighbouring countries. However, it was not an easy task to reach this goal, due to the ongoing Nagorno-Karabakh conflict, the high level of tension between Russia and Georgia, and finally, Russia's continuing view of the South Caucasus as within its sphere of influence.[279]

Even though the Turkish-led CSCP was not successful, it paved the way for rapprochement between Turkey and Armenia. The Turkish government tried to normalise relations, lift the trade embargo, and open its border with Armenia. The qualifying matches for the 2010 FIFA World Cup in September 2008 created a comprehensive framework for Turkey's new policy. Abdullah Gul, President of the Turkish Republic, visited the capital city of Armenia in order to watch the football match between the Armenian and Turkish national teams and to meet with his counterpart, Serzh Sargsyan.[280]

---

278 Ceyhun Mahmudlu and Aqil Əhmədov, ""Beş Günlük Müharibə" nin Cənubi Qafqaz Dövlətlərinə Təsiri", *Journal of Qafqaz University*, 2010: 46-47.

279 Gulshan Pashayeva, "The Nagorno Karabakh Conflict in the Aftermath of the Russia-Georgia War", *Turkish Policy Quarterly*, 8 (4), 2009: 62.

280 Araz Aslanli, "Azerbaijan-Russia Relations: Is Foreign Policy Strategy of Azerbaijan Changing?", *Turkish Policy Quarterly*, 9 (3), 2010: 143.

Turkey's hopes of negotiating the opening of the border with Armenia led to closer relations with Yerevan, through which Turkey would play a more active role in the political affairs of the South Caucasus in general and Armenia in particular.[281] Turkey believed that developing bilateral relations and opening the border would not only set the ground for peace with Armenia, but would also strengthen Turkey's diplomatic stand regarding the events of 1915—which continue to have a significant impact on Armenia and the Armenian Diaspora—and might avoid its alienation by Western countries.[282] It was also stated that, "the Turkey–Armenia Protocols were seen as important for bilateral relations not only between Ankara and Yerevan, but also between Yerevan and Baku."[283] Thus, in April 2009, Turkey issued a joint statement together with Armenia on the establishment of a comprehensive framework that will be the base for a road map.[284]

Azerbaijan welcomed these positive developments between Armenia and Turkey. However, it had some concerns relating to statements on the Armenian side. From the outset of negotiations, the Armenian authorities refused for the Nagorno-Karabakh conflict to be included in the process.[285] This declaration escalated existing fears on the Azerbaijani side, leading Azerbaijan to stress its official perspective via different channels. The spokesman of the Ministry of Foreign Affairs of Azerbaijan stated that, without doubt, every sovereign country has the right to develop bilateral cooperation with another country in accordance to their will; but the Azerbaijani side considered the normalisation of relations and the opening of the border between Armenia and Turkey, without reaching a final agreement on the Nagorno-Karabakh conflict, to be against its national interests.[286] Furthermore, on 28 April 2009, during a press conference with President of the European Commission José Manuel Barroso, President Ilham Aliyev insisted that "we, the Azerbaijani people, want to know [the] answer to one very simple question: is

281 Abilov and Isayev, "Azerbaijan-Russian Relations", 129.
282 Thomas Ambrosio, "Unfreezing the Nagorno-Karabakh Conflict? Evaluating Peacemaking Efforts under the Obama Administration", *Ethnopolitics: Formerly Global Review of Ethnopolitics*, 10 (1), 2011: 101.
283 Ambrosio, "Unfreezing the Nagorno-Karabakh Conflict?", 103.
284 Cory Welt, "To Link or Not to Link: Turkey-Armenian Normalization and the Karabakh Conflict", *Caucasus International*, 2 (1), 2012: 55.
285 Zaur Shiriyev and Celia Davies, "The Turkey-Armenia-Azerbaijan Triangle: The Unexpected Outcomes of the Zurich Protocols", *Perceptions*, 18 (1), 2013: 193.
286 Pashayeva, "The Nagorno Karabakh Conflict in the Aftermath of the Russia-Georgia War", 66.

the Nagorno-Karabakh conflict a precondition for the rapprochement process or not?"[287]

In order to dissipate Azerbaijan's concerns, during his visit to Baku in May 2009, Turkish Prime Minister Erdoğan gave assurances that there would be no progress on the border issue between Turkey and Armenia without positive steps on the Armenian side regarding to the resolution of the Nagorno-Karabakh conflict.[288] During a joint press conference with President Ilham Aliyev, Erdoğan was also clear that "there is a relation of cause and effect here. The occupation of Nagorno-Karabakh is a cause, and the closure of the border is an effect. Without the occupation ending, the gates will not be opened."[289]

On 10 October 2009 in Zurich, the rapprochement process between Turkey and Armenia reached its culmination with the signing of the two documents by the Minister of Foreign Affairs of Turkey Ahmet Davutoğlu and the Armenian Minister of Foreign Affairs Edward Nalbandyan: the Protocol on the Establishment of Diplomatic Relations; and the Protocol on the Development of Bilateral Relations."[290] According to the protocols, the border between the two countries would be opened within two months of the ratification of the document by both parliaments. No mention was made of a solution to the Nagorno-Karabakh conflict. This was seen on the Azerbaijan side as a betrayal to the key principles on which the brotherly relations between Azerbaijan and Turkey are based.[291] Azerbaijan was concerned that if the Turkish and Armenian parliaments ratified the protocols, it would end the physical isolation and economic embargo of Armenia that Azerbaijan had enforced since the outset of the conflict. Azerbaijan would then have no other choice but to compromise in the solution of the conflict, having lost its main leverage to influence negotiations on the future status of Nagorno-Karabakh. This would likely encourage the Armenian side to harden its position on the issue and prolong the status quo. Moreover, Azerbaijan's only ally in the Nagorno-Karabakh conflict would make peace with its enemy.[292]

287 Shiriyev and Davies, "The Turkey-Armenia-Azerbaijan Triangle", 192.
288 Welt, "To Link or Not to Link", 54.
289 Abilov, "The Discourse 'One Nation Two State'", 47.
290 Shiriyev and Davies, "The Turkey-Armenia-Azerbaijan Triangle", 199.
291 Kamer Kasim, "American Policy toward the Nagorno-Karabakh Conflict and Implications for its Resolution", *Journal of Muslim Minority Affairs*, 32 (2), 2012: 239.
292 Ambrosio, "Unfreezing the Nagorno-Karabakh Conflict?", 103.

In the light of these factors, Azerbaijan reacted harshly to the protocols.[293] One day before they were signed, President Ilham Aliyev stated in the CIS summit of CIS in Chișinău: "I am absolutely convinced that the resolution of the Karabakh conflict and the opening of the Turkey–Armenia border must proceed in a parallel fashion ... Between these two processes there is no official link, but an unofficial one exists. This tie must be preserved and the two questions must be resolved in a parallel fashion and at the same time."[294]A week later, Aliyev threatened to increase the price at which Azeri energy resources were sold to Turkey, noting that selling the gas to Turkey at $120 per thousand cubic meters—one-third of the market price —was not economically rational. Although the increasing gas price was explained as due to commercial factors rather that the protocols, political analysts argued that this step was a signal to Turkey that it needed to take the interests of Azerbaijan, an important energy exporter, into consideration.[295] Furthermore, on 14 October 2009, the same day that Turkish President Abdullah Gül met with Armenian President Serzh Sargsyan during a football match between the nations, the State Oil Company of the Azerbaijan Republic (SOCAR) signed a contract with Russian energy company Gazprom to supply 0.5 bcm of Azerbaijani gas annually to Russia at a rate of $350 per thousand cubic meters, while promising to increase the amount of the gas in future. By signing this agreement, Azerbaijan sent a clear message to Turkey that it is not the only country through which Azerbaijan can transport gas to market, and that it may choose Russia as its primary transit route if the Turkey–Armenia border was opened without a solution to the Nagorno-Karabakh conflict.[296]

However, despite these disputes, both Turkey and Azerbaijan were aware that increasing tensions and worsening bilateral cooperation between the states would only benefit Armenia and Russia. It was also clear to Turkey that the border opening would fundamentally damage its brotherly relations with Azerbaijan. Therefore, the Turkish side clarified

293 Fariz Ismailzade, "Turkish-Azerbaijani "Cold War:" Moscow Benefits from Washington's Indecisiveness", *Eurasia Daily Monitor*, 6 (201), 2 November 2009, accessed 12.05.2018. HTTP://WWW.JAMESTOWN.ORG/SINGLE/?NO_CACHE=1&TX_TTNEWS%5BTT_NEWS%5D=35684#.VG _Pl7uXSRJ (accessed May 22, 2018.

294 Shiriyev and Davies, "The Turkey-Armenia-Azerbaijan Triangle", 199.

295 Abilov, "The Discourse "One Nation Two State"", 48.

296 Anar Valiyev, "Finlandization or Strategy of Keeping the Balance?: Azerbaijan's Foreign Policy since the Russian-Georgian War", *PONARS Eurasia Policy Memo*, 112, 2010: 1-2.

that the development of relations with Armenia would only be possible after the withdrawal of Armenian forces from Nagorno-Karabakh.[297]

As a result, after the signing of the protocols, Turkey engaged deeply in the resolution of the Nagorno-Karabakh conflict. Accordingly, while meeting in Sochi, Prime Minister Erdoğan discussed the case with his Russian counterpart, Vladimir Putin, and urged Russia to take more responsibility for the resolution of the conflict.[298] However, the Russian leader instead insisted that the parties in the Nagorno-Karabakh dispute must find a solution. Moreover, Putin stated that the resolution of the conflict should be distinguished from the border issue and that the two disputes should be resolved separately. During his visit to the United States on 9 December 2009, Erdoğan also discussed the matter with President Barack Obama and appealed for US intervention in the resolution process. However, the meeting with Obama proved as unsuccessful as that with Putin.[299]

Alongside negotiation with the leaders of the co-chair countries of the Minsk Group, in order to achieve solution of the Nagorno-Karabakh conflict, there was also the issue of the ratification of the protocols. The parliaments of both Turkey and Armenia were required to ratify the protocols to enable them to come into force. As a result of the strong reaction of Azerbaijan and the failure of negotiation attempts with the presidents of Russia and the United States, Turkey was unable to ratify the protocols. Therefore, Turkey was forced to seek a resolution to the Nagorno-Karabakh conflict before opening the border with Armenia. Losing Azerbaijan was not a price that Turkey wanted to pay to establish bilateral relations with Armenia. In contrast, the Constitutional Court of Armenia, which examines all international treaties before ratification by parliament, approved the protocols, but put forward three preconditions:

1. The Republic of Armenia stands in support of the task of achieving international recognition of the 1915 Genocide in Ottoman Turkey and Western Armenia, as regulated by the Constitution of the Republic of Armenia and the Armenian Declaration of Independence.

2. It rejected any connection between the new agreement with Turkey and the Nagorno-Karabakh issue.

---

297 Ibrahimov, "Turkish-Azerbaijani Relations and Turkey's Policy in the Central Asia", 18.
298 Rovshan Ibrahimov, "Turkish-Armenian Rapprochement: Defining the Process and Its Impact on Relations between Azerbaijan and Turkey", *Caspian Report*, 6, 2014: 93-94.
299 Ibrahimov, "Turkish-Armenian Rapprochement", 94.

3. The implementation of the protocols did not imply Armenia's official recognition of the existing Turkey–Armenia border, established by the 1921 Treaty of Kars.[300]

The Armenian side also rejected "the mutual recognition of the existing border between the two countries as defined by relevant treaties of international law," a premise of the protocols.[301] Under such conditions, Turkey could not ratify the protocols and invest in the realisation of a regional stability policy if other partners of the CSCP and world powers with interests in the South Caucasus were unwilling to pay the price for peace in the region. Therefore, Turkey gradually returned to its closed border policy with Armenia and instead focused on strengthening its bilateral ties with Azerbaijan.

Post-Protocol Political and Economic Developments between Two Countries

Since the summer of 2010, relations between Turkey and Azerbaijan have entered a new stage. During the visit of Turkish President Abdulla Gul to Baku that August, the two countries signed a new Agreement on Strategic Partnership and Mutual Support. The treaty was considered an indirect response to the military agreement between Russia and Armenia. The Turkish–Azerbaijani agreement was a sign of solidarity between the states and calculated to strengthen relations further, in order to counter Russian presence in the region.[302] Subsequently, President of Russia Dmitry Medvedev signed a deal with President Sargsyan of Armenia on 20 August 2010 in Yerevan, to extend the Russian military base in Gumri for an additional twenty-four years. The existing treaty between Russia and Armenia was due to last until 2020, but this new deal extended it until 2044. According to this agreement, Russia was also obliged to modernise the Armenian military units, effectively making Russia a guarantor of the security of Armenia. This may lead to significant negative consequences for the Nagorno-Karabakh conflict and hinder a possible intervention by Turkey

---

300 Abilov, "The Discourse 'One Nation Two State'", 50.
301 Nona Mikhelidze, "The Turkish-Armenian Rapprochement at the Deadlock", *DOCUMENTI IAI*, 10 (05), 2010: 3.
302 Tracey German, "The Nagorno-Karabakh Conflict between Azerbaijan and Armenia: Security Issues in the Caucasus", *Journal of Muslim Minority Affairs*, 32 (2), 2012: 222.

in favour of Azerbaijan.[303] The parliament of Azerbaijan ratified the Agreement on Strategic Partnership and Mutual Support on 21 December, with it set to continue until 2020 with the option for a further 10-year extension if both parties are willing.[304]

In September 2010, Turkey and Azerbaijan signed another deal, for the establishment of a high-level bilateral Strategic Cooperation Council, that intended to increase cooperation between the two states even further. According to the agreement, if a third party attacked either side the countries should provide military assistance to each other. The treaty also stated that the parties are obliged to strengthen "military-technical cooperation, arms supply and the establishment of infrastructure for possible joint operations in the future."[305]

Along with security issues, in 2011 Azerbaijan and Turkey entered a significant new period in energy cooperation, which encouraged both parties to develop bilateral partnerships in the gas sector and transportation routes. After a long negotiation, the countries launched TANAP in 2011, in place of the failed Nabucco pipeline. The construction of TANAP began in March 2015 and it was put into operation in June 2018, creating a new dimension to the bilateral relations between Azerbaijan and Turkey. The pipeline will carry 16 bcm of natural gas annually to the European market through Turkey.[306] The shareholders of TANAP are SOCAR, BP, and the Turkish government, which possess 58%, 12%, and 30% shares of the project, respectively. TANAP is considered as a significant contribution to the overall energy policy of Turkey. Initially, by the realisation of this project, Turkey will receive a large amount of natural gas for its domestic market at a favourable price. In addition, it will help Turkey to diversify its energy strategy, in order to decrease its dependence on Russia and give leverage in future energy negotiations with Russia and Iran for the import of natural gas for domestic use. Meanwhile, it constitutes a significant step in the realisation of Turkey's ambition to be an energy hub between East and West. It should also be noted that the selection of the Trans Adriatic Pipeline (TAP) as the follow-up project of TANAP was another significant transportation route that is being

---

303 Rasizade, "Azerbaijan's Prospects in Nagorno-Karabakh", 89.
304 Shahin Abbasov, "Azerbaijan-Turkey Military Pact Signals Impatience with Minsk Talks", *EUR-ASIANET.org*, 18 January, 2011, accessed 28.05.2018, http://www.eurasianet.org/node/62732.
305 German, "The Nagorno-Karabakh Conflict between Azerbaijan and Armenia", 222.
306 Kemal Kirişçi and Andrew Moffatt, "Turkey and the South Caucasus: An Opportunity for Soft Regionalism?", *Regional Security Issues*, 2015: 73.

implemented by Azerbaijan and Turkey, further strengthening cooperation between the two states and making both important players in the energy security of Europe.[307]

As already mentioned, the transportation network has also played a great role in the development of bilateral economic and strategic relations between the two states. The construction of the Baku–Tbilisi–Kars Railway, which increases the percentage of commodities carried by the Transport Corridor Europe–Caucasus–Asia (TRACECA), which connects China with the European market, is another significant project that will increase the transit potential of both countries.[308]

Generally speaking, economic relations plays a significant role in the relations between the two countries. Since the establishment of bilateral relations in the first years of the 1990s, Azerbaijan and Turkey have deepened their economic cooperation through bilateral trades, foreign direct investment, and the aforementioned energy projects. Various agreements have also been signed by the governments of Azerbaijan and Turkey, which set out the legal and institutional mechanisms for carrying out bilateral economic relations. Trade and economic agreements between two countries are as follows:

- Trade, Economic and Technical Cooperation Agreement – 1992
- Prevention of Double Taxing Agreement – 1994
- Mutual Promotion and Protection of Investments Agreement – 1995
- Intergovernmental Joint Economic Commission Meetings Protocols (KEK)
  - KEK I. Term – 1997
  - KEK II. Term – 2001
  - KEK III. Term – 2005
  - KEK IV. Term – 2006
  - KEK V. Term – 2008
  - KEK VI. Term – 2011[309]
  - KEK VII. Term – 2014[310]

---

307 Şaban Kardaş, "The Turkey-Azerbaijan Energy Partnership in the Context of the Southern Corridor", *Istituto Affari Internazionali Working Papers*, 14, 2014: 7-8.
308 Kirişçi and Moffatt, "Turkey and the South Caucasus", 73.
309 Yesevi and Tiftikcigil, "Turkey-Azerbaijan Energy Relations", 37.
310 Araz Aslanlı, "Türkiye-Azerbaycan Ekonomik İlişkileri", *YÖNETİM VE EKONOMI*, 25(1), 2018: 27.

In terms of economic cooperation in non-energy sectors, Turkey was one of the first countries to invest in Azerbaijan. There are 1,685 registered companies originating in Turkey that operate in the Azerbaijani market.[311] The amount of Turkish capital invested in Azerbaijan is approximately $4.7 billion, and around one-third of this capital is invested in non-energy areas,[312] mainly in the infrastructure, construction, transportation, telecommunications, tourism, education, bakery, textiles, and furniture sectors.[313]

Meanwhile, Azerbaijan is also one of the most important investors in Turkey, with more than 1,000 investment companies of Azerbaijani origin operating in Turkey. The overall investment of these companies currently amounts to $5 billion, and it is expected to reach $20 billion by 2020.[314] SOCAR is one of the most important foreign companies to operate in Turkey, and by acquiring the main share of Petkim, the largest petrochemical company in Turkey, SOCAR has increased its investment in the country. Today, SOCAR's involvement in various significant investment projects in Turkey make it one of the biggest foreign direct investors in the Turkish market, totalling $17 billion of investments.[315] The table below (see Table 1) charts the volume of trade between the two countries from 1992 to 2016, showing an increase from approximately $200 million to $2.5 billion between these years.

Conclusion

All of these transportation networks and energy projects, economic cooperation, and the strategic partnership between Azerbaijan and Turkey, indicate that relations between the countries are based not only on cultural and linguistic proximity, ethnic kinship, and ideological brotherhood, as was the case during the first decades of their diplomatic engagement. Current relations instead remain based on geopolitical realities. Since

---

311 Serhat Yüksel, Shahriyar Mukhtarov, Ceyhun Mahmudlu, Jeyhun I. Mikayilov and Anar Iskandarov, "Measuring International Migration in Azerbaijan", *Sustainability*, 10(132), 2018: 6.

312 Mitat Çelikpala and Cavid Veliyev, "Azerbaijan-Georgia-Turkey: An Example of a Successful Regional Cooperation", *Center for International and European Studies Policy Brief*, 4, 2015: 13.

313 Şaban Kardaş and Fatih Macit, "Turkey-Azerbaijan Relations: The Economic Dimensions", *Journal of Caspian Affairs*, 1 (1), 2015: 27.

314 Çelikpala and Veliyev, "Azerbaijan-Georgia-Turkey", 13.

315 Kardaş and Macit, "Turkey-Azerbaijan Relations", 41-42.

2009, the failure of the Turkish CSCP and the collapse of the protocols regarding the rapprochement of Turkey and Armenia and the opening of the border between the two states show that Azerbaijan and Turkey need each other more than any states in the region, in order to implement their foreign policy priorities in regards to energy, economy, and security. Thus, today's bilateral relations and mutual cooperation between Azerbaijan and Turkey in all the aforementioned spheres will continue to develop and both countries will preserve this development for their own benefit.

Table 1. Trade Volume between Azerbaijan and Turkey (Million $)

Years	Export from Turkey	Import to Turkey	Trade volume
1992	87,107.0	125,617.0	214,716.0
1993	63,635.0	60,569.0	126,197.0
1994	76,027.0	16,463.0	94,484.0
1995	140,510.2	26,445.0	168,950.0
1996	216,257.8	39,048.8	257,302.2
1997	179,701.8	41,283.1	222,981.9
1998	219,688.8	135,837.8	357,524.6
1999	142,991.2	69,086.8	214,077.0
2000	128,502.6	104,981.0	235,483.6
2001	148,167.4	67,381.6	217,550.0
2002	156,218.7	83,396.5	241,617.2
2003	195,252.0	107,036.0	303,291.0
2004	224,967.8	182,621.6	409,593.4
2005	313,001.6	275,959.3	590,956.9
2006	385,040.2	388,144.8	775,191.0
2007	624,572.5	1,056,323.0	1,682,903.0
2008	807,168.9	626,157.2	1,435,334.0
2009	906,984.2	107,620.0	1,016,613.0
2010	771,442.4	170,893.7	944,346.1
2011	1,302,443.1	455,761.0	1,760,215.0
2012	1,520,405.1	600,025.1	2,120,430.2
2013	1,463,804.9	525,985.8	1,989,790.7
2014	1,286,641.4	502,492.8	1,789,134.2
2015	1,171,385.4	1,477,256.7	2,648,642.1
2016	1,181,578.4	1,132,820.0	2,314,398.4

Source: The State Statistical Committee of the Republic of Azerbaijan[316]

---

316 Table retrieved from Aslanlı, "Türkiye-Azerbaycan Ekonomik İlişkileri", 23.

CHAPTER 6
The Next Front? Iranian Ambitions and Azerbaijan's Strategic Bulwark

Mitchell Belfer

Introduction

European scholarship tends to view geopolitics as archaic. However, the abandonment of geopolitical planning remains an elusive luxury for the vast majority of states across the Caucasus, Middle East, and Central Asia. The recent tidal wave of terrorism, war, and insurgency are reminders that ensuring national survival requires actionable decision-making, not abstract theories.

Baku does not harbour many illusions.

At the best of times, the South Caucasus is a dangerous region.[317] With its two local allies preoccupied—Turkey vis-à-vis Syria and Georgia vis-à-vis Russia—and its international partners in Europe and the United States increasingly unreliable, Azerbaijan is being forced to navigate a new, more turbulent, path. Russia may have reduced its Caspian ambitions (for now), but it remains a looming, largely unpredictable, actor—neither ally nor adversary. Left alone to recalibrate its geopolitical orientation, Baku has sought to relieve tensions with Armenia by opening up to Iran. Yet, for all the energies Baku has invested in engaging with the Islamic Republic, Iran remains a steadfast ally of Yerevan, and has not budged on its antagonistic position related to the Azerbaijan-Armenia conflict over the latter's occupation of Nagorno-Karabakh. Tehran keeps the embers burning. The deep-freeze between Baku and Yerevan is

---

317 For a definition of "dangerous region," see: Mitchell Belfer, *Small State, Dangerous Region: A Strategic Assessment of Bahrain*, Frankfurt: Peter Lang Publishing, 2014, 163–7.

facilitating the growth in power and influence of Iran in the Caspian Sea region. Iran seeks hegemony—and not only in the Middle East. Azerbaijan remains a thorn in Iran's ambitions. Autarkic in security provisions, Baku is sensitive to its geopolitical surroundings, and those dynamics largely determine the country's strategic priorities and, importantly, its present solutions.

This chapter analyses Baku's geopolitical options from a theoretical perspective. While Azerbaijan retains an assortment of policy tools in its toolbox, this work recognises three paths that *could* be undertaken: hegemony, neutrality, or alliance. At the outset, it dismisses two.

Reaching for hegemony in the South Caucasus is not a viable policy option for Azerbaijan. The region is too riven with competition, too fractious, too penetrated to facilitate the rise of any one, dominant power. Instead, the region is defined by a balance of power system that uses extended deterrence to limit entrepreneurial behaviours. Iran is the wild card in this scenario, and while it is not the only revisionist actor, it remains the only state in the South Caucasus to harbour interests in regional and trans-regional hegemony. This is because Iran's Twelver ideology calls for the exportation of Islamic revolution along *all* of its frontiers (into Azerbaijan, Turkmenistan, Bahrain, Saudi Arabia, Iraq, etc.). So, while the other regional actors remain balance-focused, Iran alone seeks to upend the existing order and emerge as hegemon. As this chapter illustrates, such hegemonic aspirations may actually produce the opposite and instead spark a robust movement against it. Certainly, Azerbaijan retains the hard power to subdue Armenia and the soft power to charm Georgia—but it does not maintain the ambition to impose itself. It remains primarily focused on recovering occupied territories from Armenian control, but it does not seek to occupy Armenia itself. In short, Azerbaijan does not, and will not, seek hegemony.

Neutrality is also not an option. Proximity to centres of power reduces Baku's freedom of movement. It cannot disengage. It will never become Sweden. While there is a case for Azerbaijan to develop some form of armed neutrality—along the Swiss model—given the geopolitical arrangements in the region, it is unlikely to work. Switzerland survived two World Wars by being able to retreat into its mountains and, with clockwork efficiency, deploy its armed forces to defensive positions. Had Nazi Germany invaded, it simply would have destroyed the roads and commenced a war of attrition—awaiting the arrival of the Allied forces. Azerbaijan is being squeezed between the Armenian–Iranian pincer, and neutrality is unlikely to be honoured. Instead, history suggests that in the South Caucasus, offensive states gain the advantage—there are few protective retreats, despite the high mountains that clot the region. And, unlike Switzerland, Azerbaijan's geography is too diverse to develop a single *modus operandi* for security provisions: mountains, open sea, and flatlands each present unique challenges—points further addressed below.

Only by enhancing an alliance network with exogenous powers can Azerbaijan survive in its region: by outflanking its more aggressive rivals and reinforcing second and even third fronts, in order to provide Baku with additional strategic options, while generating a more robust balancing capability and, through it, gaining important breathing space.

However, since Azerbaijan's main rival is Iran, Baku's ability to enlist allies that share its threat perception (for example, regarding the Arab Gulf states and Israel) will likely generate a wider, regional security dilemma, since Azerbaijan's outflanking may raise the (mis)perception in Tehran, Yerevan and, probably, Moscow, that Baku is attempting to enhance its regional position at their expense.[318] In other words, the rapid construction of an alliance system will enhance Azerbaijan's power but may, simultaneously, reduce its security, since its rival (Iran) and adversary (Armenia) would likely attempt to disrupt Baku's new-found partnerships before the relationships are consolidated. This work suggests that Azerbaijan should attempt to form alliances with Arab Gulf states— particularly Saudi Arabia, Bahrain, and the United Arab Emirates—since they share similar threat perceptions of Iran and are, together, able to construct a workable system of deterrence to limit and rollback the expansionist policies of the Islamic Republic.

This chapter addresses the question of how Azerbaijan can overcome its geopolitical vulnerabilities—via alliance—without sparking conflict. The subsequent analysis maintains that, while it would be inappropriate to relegate armed conflict as impossible, the likelihood of conflict diminishes as deterrent capabilities are enhanced. Functioning alliances produce credible deterrence, and hence alliance is preferable to other policy strands in geopolitically-sensitive regions. Before continuing, it is important to identify the specific details of Azerbaijan's geopolitical situation,

---

318 This work recognises Iran as Azerbaijan's main regional rival. Armenia is a flashpoint, not a rival. The imbalance of power in favour of Azerbaijan is too great for Armenia to confront it itself and recruits allies — such as the Islamic Republic — to support its endeavours since Iran is a rival.

in order to better grasp the nature of its challenges and rivalries, and the dimensions of its security policies that work at overcoming these.

Azerbaijan's Geopolitical Situation

Since Azerbaijan's earliest history, four key geographic features have helped define its place in the region and the wider international community. These are:

1. the country's protective ring of mountains
2. the pincer river system of the Araxes and Kura, which provides fresh water for agriculture and consumption, food-stocks, hydroelectricity capabilities, and (previously) access to more distant places (navigation)
3. arable land for agriculture in the range of some 15–18%
4. the seaboard of the Caspian Sea (some 713 kilometres), which connects Azerbaijan to Russia, Kazakhstan, Turkmenistan, and Iran.

These features deserve deeper analysis, since they serve to (partially) determine Azerbaijan's interests and behaviour.

Mountains—Three ranges embrace Azerbaijan: the Greater Caucasus, which form part of the border with Georgia and Russia; the Lower Caucasus, shared with Armenia; and the Talysh, along much of the Iranian frontier. It is important to remember that mountains are not neutral territories, and neither are they some form of "no man's land" or natural buffer areas. Mountains are of vital strategic importance, and states have traditionally expended tremendous national energies attempting to gain high grounds, as natural gateways and ramparts. In the Caucasus, many of the current conflicts are based on mountain boundaries, and one of the main reasons for this work's proposal that Azerbaijan shift to a more Arab-focused flank to outmanoeuvre Iran, is based on Iranian control over vital mountainous regions which could be used as pressure points in their dyadic relationship. Vying to secure their share of the mountain ranges, while preventing others from doing so, is a vital, defining, interest of Azerbaijan, no matter the century or the political orientation of its leadership.

Rivers—While some twenty-five notable rivers criss-cross Azerbaijani territory, it is the flow of the Araxes (Araz) and the Kura (Mt'k'vari) that has risen to geopolitical significance for Azerbaijan (and the other riparian states); since these, together, form the country's most important sources of potable water (especially the Kura), are a significant source of foodstuffs, and provide hydroelectric power potential. While it falls beyond the scope of this work to detail the specific geographic contributions that these rivers have made to Azerbaijan's geopolitical decision-making, it is important to remember that both retain their own basins, and the each basin helps to water the country's agricultural sector. Hence, the Araxes and Kura basins—and the rivers running through them—bear direct socio-economic and material significance for the communities that rely on them and, by extension, geopolitical significance for the state. The Araxes forms a huge portion of the Iran–Azerbaijan border; it is political by its very nature. Since these rivers flow through most of the Caucasus countries—the Araxes flows through Turkey, Azerbaijan, Armenia, and Iran; and the Kura flows through Turkey, Georgia, and Azerbaijan—they may act as geopolitical tools.

Upstream states can use water flows to pressure downstream states (as with Turkey's control of the headwaters of the Tigris and Euphrates), and therefore increase downstream states' sense of vulnerability. Since both of these rivers are predominately within Azerbaijan's territory, it has been more sensitive to the way others use them, and has spent considerable diplomatic energy ensuring that upstream states do not interrupt water flows. In terms of this assessment—to explain why Azerbaijan should seek to outflank Iran by investing politically in the Arabian Gulf—the Araxes and Kura should be understood in two ways. First, the Araxes river–border is more a symbolic division than a material one, and since the USSR's Cold War industrial projects all but drained the river, the boundary is rather porous. Iran is more capable of exerting pressure on Azerbaijan than the inverse. For Azerbaijan to rebalance the pressure on Iran, it needs to move beyond their shared frontiers. Secondly, it is also worth noting that potable water in Iran is on the decline owing to poor infrastructure, sanctions, and a policy black hole: the Islamic Republic is facing an acute water crisis. Since Azerbaijan is water-rich and Iran is increasingly water-poor, the latter may have an additional incentive to attempt to seize Azerbaijani water sources, especially as Iran's demographic boom continues apace. Again, for Azerbaijan to prevent this, it could—as discussed in greater detail below—consolidate its relationship with the Gulf States, to balance against the Islamic Republic.

Arable Land—Similar to its water resources, Azerbaijan maintains an abundance of arable land as a percentage of its total landmass. This implies that Azerbaijan could be autarkic in the production of foodstuffs and has increased the geopolitical value of its territory. With environmental challenges unfolding at a heightened pace, states seek to control adequate food production capabilities, and arable land has come again to represent an important geopolitical resource. In the wider Caucasus region, only Turkey (26.7%) has managed to enhance its arable lands to a greater degree than Azerbaijan (22.8%). Each of Azerbaijan's identified adversaries has a significantly lower percentage of arable land (Iran 10.8%, Russia 7.4%, and Armenia 15.1%).[319] This is particularly detrimental to Iran, since the country is facing a population boom and will thus require additional foodstuffs, just as urbanisation continues to draw people away from more rural communities. Moreover, the looming return of sanctions—following the United States's decision to abandon the Joint Comprehensive Plan of Action, aka the Iran Nuclear Deal—is set to further frustrate Iranian food production. So, much like the situation related to water, Azerbaijan will need to counteract Iran's growing appetite by reinforcing its strategic position vis-à-vis the Islamic Republic. For Armenia, arable land is a less important geopolitical item since it is a small, self-sufficient, rural state.

The Caspian Sea—The world's largest lake, in surface and volume, is one of the most important geopolitical areas in contemporary international relations, owing to the states that share it and the riches buried beneath its seabed. Specifically, and to put the Caspian Sea region into context, "the EIA estimates that there were 48 billion barrels of oil and 292 trillion cubic feet of natural gas in proved and probable reserves within the basins that make up the Caspian Sea and surrounding area."[320] As a result, control over the Caspian Sea, and its littoral, has emerged as a key interest for local and international powers alike. For Azerbaijan, this has been a mixed blessing, since it has implied a steady flow of allies and adversaries. Unfortunately, however, none of Azerbaijan's allies share the littoral; Georgia and Turkey—Azerbaijan's only regional allies—are Black Sea states, while its other partners are located in more distant regions. So, Azerbaijan shares the Caspian Sea with one adversary (Iran), retains frosty relations with another (Turkmenistan), while remaining engaged in a "wait-and-see" situation with Russia. At the same

---

319 See "Arable Land", *The World Bank*, 2017, accessed 12.05.2018, http://data.worldbank.org/indicator /AG.LND.ARBL.ZS.

320 US Energy Information Administration, "Oil and Natural Gas Production is Growing in Caspian Sea Region", 11 September 2013, accessed 02.06.2018, https://www.eia.gov/todayinenergy /detail.cfm?id=12911.

time, Baku's relationship to Kazakhstan is deeply problematic, since the latter is orbiting Russia's sphere of influence and has very little room to manoeuvre. In this context, it is clear that the Caspian Sea acts as a source of Azerbaijan's geopolitical strength—much of the state's national wealth is derived from Sea-related resources and its international alliances are a reflection of its geopolitical position—as well as its ultimate vulnerability, since its adversaries are lined-up along the littoral. Azerbaijan retains neither the capabilities nor interests to dominate the Caspian Sea or its environs. Instead, it seeks to maintain a legitimate exclusive economic zone (EEZ), so that it may add many of the Sea's hydrocarbon resources to its national coffers. Iran, however, is attempting to project its power around the Sea, and hence Azerbaijan's geopolitical strategy is based on bringing exogenous powers into the region, in order to prevent it from being hijacked by Tehran. Iran's periodic interference with Azerbaijani research vessels in the Caspian Sea (including shootings) reminds Baku that Tehran's deployment of armed force remains a possibility.

Before turning to the types of alliances that Azerbaijan may pursue to enhance its deterrent capability vis-à-vis Iran, it is essential to lay bare the main geopolitical challenges that currently preoccupy Baku. For the most part these have not changed since "Baku suddenly emerged in the 1890s as the world's oil capital."[321] However, they serve as one of the foundations for strategic decision-making in the country, and therefore need further presentation and understanding.

Azerbaijan's Main Geopolitical Challenges: The Iran and Armenia Axis

Three identifiable geopolitical challenges currently face Azerbaijan—and they all involve Iran and Armenia.

First, there is the very real possibility of **encirclement** and, with encirclement, the possibility of the enforcement of an economic embargo or quarantine of Azerbaijan—especially in its hydrocarbons trade. With Georgia (Azerbaijan's only allied neighbour) under continued Russian pressure and plagued by internal paralysis, Armenia bent on maintaining its Nagorno-Karabakh proxy, and Iran steadily increasing its Central Asian presence, Azerbaijan's international access is becoming more and

---

321   Karl E. Meyer, *The Dust of Empire*, The Century Foundation, New York: USA, 2003, 164.

more restricted, and its constraints increasingly apparent. This is a joint Armenian–Iranian challenge.[322]

Second, as noted above, there is a "northern push," strategically and demographically, from Iran. Instead of being satisfied with the existing status quo of an encircled Azerbaijan, it is clear that Iran is trying to break through to its north and on the Caspian Sea. Azerbaijan has recognised this challenge and, already in 2013, developed its own Maritime Security Strategy (MSS) that is designed for "enhancing border protection and tackling possible threats to [its] hydrocarbon fields, wells, production facilities, and underwater pipeline systems in the Caspian Sea."[323] So far, this has deterred Iranian manoeuvres—but for how long?

Finally, as in other parts of the post-Soviet space, Azerbaijan needs to remain vigilant against low-intensity operations aimed at slicing away parts of its national territory (so-called salami tactics). There are no sizeable, mobilisable language-minorities in the country (unlike in Ukraine or Georgia), or disgruntled cultural-political groups (such as in Georgia, vis-à-vis Abkhazia and South Ossetia), or even "marginalised" Shia communities (as Iran's false narratives of the Arab Gulf states suggest). Nonetheless, Iran continues to eye Azerbaijan—and especially its energy fields—and has supported Armenia's seizure of Nagorno-Karabakh. The Islamic Republic has also ensured that Baku's supply links to the Nakhchivan Autonomous Republic are monitored and remain a pressure point, to be exploited by Tehran at will. Even the current political situation in Yerevan is not moderating Iran's relationship to Armenia, but rather reinforcing an Iranian–Armenian axis that is more able to rally pressure against Baku in pursuit of their interests. Additionally, it is not impossible for Iran to ignite sectarianism or radicalise people in Azerbaijan in an attempt to heighten national tensions and score geopolitical points against Azerbaijan in the process.[324]

Since there are clearly three main challenges facing Azerbaijan that stem from the Iranian–Armenian axis, and given that Iran is clearly

322 For a reading into regional — re: South Caucasus — tensions and the origins of the modern Azerbaijan-Iran relationship, including drivers of tensions, see: Abdollah Baei Iashaki, Masoumeh Rad Goudarzi and Davood Amraei (2013), 'The Roots of Tension in the South Caucasus: The Case of Iran-Azerbaijan Relationship,' *Journal of Politics and Law*, 6:4.

323 Peter Dunai, "Azerbaijan Inaugurates Shipyard", *IHS Jane's Defence Weekly*, 51 (31), 30 July 2014, 20.

324 Iran also stands accused of adding additional 'administrative pressure' (re: repression) against its own, sizeable ethnic Azerbaijani population. For information about this see: John R Bradley, "Iran's Ethnic Tinderbox," *The Washington Quarterly*, 30, 2007: 181-190.

Baku's more potent adversary (Armenia would not be able to deter Azerbaijan without the support of the Islamic Republic), it may be prudent to pay more attention to analysing new strategic thinking for Azerbaijan vis-à-vis Iran. After all, containing the country may assist in solving Azerbaijan's main geopolitical challenges.

On the surface, exacerbating existing Iranian–Azerbaijani tensions may seem counterproductive. However, this work suggests that since Azerbaijan is not a great regional or international power, and remains relatively small compared to Russia, Iran, and (allied) Turkey—though it is considerably more powerful than Armenia—it is unable to comprehensively deal with each of its challenges simultaneously. Instead, it is forced to deal with them on a case-by-case basis. Azerbaijan should prioritise the containment of Iran, since it seems to pose the greatest threat, and solving its Iranian challenge may heighten Azerbaijan's deterrence capabilities in general and its coercion capabilities vis-à-vis Armenia more specifically. In short, by dealing properly with Iran, Azerbaijan would also enhance its security vis-à-vis Armenia, without having to resort to armed conflict. While Armenia will likely remain an adversary of Azerbaijan, Iran is the most dangerous for the time being and Azerbaijan must take preventive action to better secure itself against the Islamic Republic.

This threat assessment is due to several overlapping features.

First—Iran is an expansionist power. While the Islamic Republic has done much over the past decade or so to adopt a tech/media-savvy approach that has generated international sympathy and garnished support for its foreign policy, its actions speak volumes. For instance, Iranian Foreign Minister, Mohammad Javad Zarif, has candidly verified the country's strategic goals, by noting that "beyond its borders, Iran seeks to enhance its regional and global stature; to promote its ideals, including Islamic democracy; to expand its bilateral and multilateral relations, particularly with neighbouring Muslim-majority countries and non-aligned states; to reduce tensions and manage disagreements with other states; to foster peace and security at both the regional and international levels through positive engagement; and to promote international understanding through dialogue and cultural understanding."[325] While Zarif intended to assuage international fears, his depiction of a chief

325 Mohammad Javad Zarif, "What Iran Really Wants: Iranian Foreign Policy in the Rouhani Era", *Foreign Affairs*, 93 (3), May/June 2014: 49.

Iranian priority being the promotion of its ideals beyond its frontiers is less than comforting, given that such ideals are based on a lethal brew of sectarianism, chauvinism, and theocratic governance. A quick glance at how those ideals have affected the regional situation stand in testament to the nature of Iranian interference, since it "seems unlikely that Iran seeks to conquer any of its neighbours outright [...] it seems more likely that Iran seeks to ensure that all of the region's governments are friendly to it and subservient."[326]

Second—Iran is ideologically driven and does not typically play by the geopolitical Westphalian rules of statecraft. Iran is not only seeking an enhanced geopolitical position; it is seeking to export its Islamic republic-esque ideological structures, implying that, if successfully implemented, Azerbaijan faces a fundamental and existential threat from Iran.

Third—There is an intimidating imbalance of power between Azerbaijan and Iran, stemming from access to key material power resources, relative GDP and GNP compared to arms production and procurement, size and strength of the armed forces, and territorial and population size. While Azerbaijan is more consolidated in terms of nationalism and trust in state institutions and leaders, Iran's ruling theocratic cabal—married to the Islamic Revolutionary Guard Corps—ensures that the Ayatollah's grip on Iran remains clenched.

Fourth—There is a sizeable ethnic Azerbaijani population in Iran—which comprises some 40 percent of the total population. The Islamic Republic is particularly sensitive to changes to the balance of power within the dyad, implying that, in this case, it remains an intrusive, status quo actor—one that Azerbaijan is required to counteract in order to enhance its strategic position in the region.

Finally—In addition to the ethnic Azerbaijanis which live in Iran, a sizable chunk of Azerbaijani territory is occupied by the Islamic Republic, which will likely take preventive actions in order to prevent its return.

---

326 Kenneth M. Pollack, *Unthinkable: Iran, the Bomb and American Strategy*, Simon and Schuster, New York: USA, 2013, 11.

Breaking the Rhythm: Solving Azerbaijan's Geopolitical Challenges

At the beginning of this chapter, three options were presented for Azerbaijan to comprehensively deal with Iran: hegemony, neutrality, or alliance. While two were dismissed out of hand, it may be useful to revisit them and to conclude with a brief assessment of Azerbaijan's alliance capability. This final section provides a wind-down in relation to Azerbaijan's geopolitical options.

While Azerbaijan lacks the political will to assert itself to the levels required to assume regional hegemony, it should be remembered that being relatively small in a particular region does not, automatically, relegate a state to the second tier of regional or international stewardship. Azerbaijan has the financial means, healthy institutions, consolidated body politic, international alliances, modern armed forces, food and potable water autarky, and stable demographic situation needed to more comprehensively assert itself along the Caspian littoral and emerge as a regional great power. This would not occur in a vacuum, however, and Azerbaijan has sought to maintain a secure regional political environment, instead of altering the balance of power for its own power aggrandisement. It recognises that any considerable Caspian power projections from Baku would produce increased tensions along the littoral and potentially lead to open hostilities. So, Azerbaijan's decision not to pursue great power status is largely rooted in its national desire to prevent greater regional instability. This may seem odd considering that Baku's most potent rival, Iran, remains undeterred from reaching for hegemony by the same logic, while Azerbaijan has adopted a strategy (alliance) that is much less antagonising. With Iran actively seeking regional hegemony, Azerbaijan's attempts at the same objective would likely spark a region-wide arms race and, ultimately, war. In such a situation, Azerbaijan would be at a severe disadvantage, considering that two of its chief adversaries are located along the littoral, while a third is proximate. Baku is striving for balance.

At the same time—and to reiterate—Azerbaijan does not have the luxury of being able to follow a posture of neutrality; the region is far too dangerous. Sure, Azerbaijan could attempt to follow in the footsteps of Switzerland (armed neutrality) or Sweden (allied neutrality), but the costs would be too great since such a posture would be seen as an intrinsic national weakness by its more entrepreneurial neighbours, inviting interference. The violation of Belgium's neutrality, prior to the outbreak of hostilities in the First World War, acts as a constant reminder of the risks associated with neutrality in periods that favour offensive strategies, where the main actors view others' neutrality as a licence to intervene. The Caucasus is unforgiving, and maintaining an offensive posture is often the only way to produce stability and enhance national defence. This is particularly true since Iran is Azerbaijan's chief adversary and would likely not respect Azerbaijani neutrality. This assumption is based on the Islamic Republic's past record of interference in Bahrain, the UAE, Kuwait, Yemen, Saudi Arabia, Iraq, Lebanon, Israel, Palestine, Afghanistan, Syria, Pakistan, and Azerbaijan.

So, since Azerbaijan is not attempting to emerge as a great regional power or hegemon, and given that adopting a neutral posture would be too risky, there is an air of determinism to Azerbaijan's security position—it must attempt to balance emergent threats via alliance. However, localised alliances are difficult to form and even more difficult to maintain, owing to the fluidity of the region and the great powers present. Azerbaijan is situated on the wrong side of the prevailing alliance network in the region. It is therefore a priority that it develop alliances with states situated beyond the Caucasus, that are able to assist it in achieving its regional goals of (in the worst case) deterring Iran, and preventing its collective action with Armenia against its interests; or (in the best case) creating disharmony within that nexus. In short, Azerbaijan requires international allies for dealing with its regional challenges.

While much ink has been spilt in suggesting the consolidation of the Israeli–Azerbaijani alliance—and this work does recognise an intrinsic value, for Azerbaijan, in such a relationship—there is another, more complete set of strategic relations that could be usefully developed in order to heighten the deterrence capability against the Islamic Republic and, if need be, to rollback Tehran's trans-regional hegemonic ambitions. An Arab-Azerbaijani Alliance Framework (A3F) could greatly enhance Azerbaijan's security position in its region, as well as its influence in the world. Now that Saudi–Russian tensions in respect to Syria/oil have subsided, the opportunity is available to create such an alliance, without instigating Moscow. The A3F would initially include Saudi Arabia, Bahrain, the UAE, Egypt, and Azerbaijan, but also be open for others to join in the future. It would be strictly a military/security alliance, with a supreme council made up of representatives from all allied states, with the sole purpose of defence cooperation. While such an alliance could be mobilised for an assortment of tasks—ranging from combatting terrorism (including terror finance) and the war on drugs, to interdicting small arms smuggling and a host of others—its main focus would be on reinventing the geopolitical situation of both Azerbaijan and the Arab states. Instead of being outflanked by the Islamic Republic, as at present, this alliance would turn the tables and develop a pincer around Iran: by generating two fronts along Iran's western and northern frontiers, and hemming it in.

It is a sad, but accurate, commentary that the Ayatollah's revolutionary Iran only understands the language of power and force. Since Azerbaijan shares the concerns of many of the Arab Gulf states when it comes to Iran, there is scope also to share the burden of deterring it and ensuring that it is unable to fulfil its hegemonic ambitions. While this chapter has focused on theoretically presenting the essence of the geopolitical challenges facing Azerbaijan, it intends to illustrate that there are practical steps that may be taken to overcome these. The view from Baku is of guarded alert so that it may continue to navigate the dangerous currents of political life in the South Caucasus.

CHAPTER 7
Emerging Strategic Partnership between Azerbaijan and Saudi Arabia: Azerbaijan's Policy of Overcoming Geography and Common Incentives

Lucie Švejdová

Introduction

Due to its geopolitical disposition, alliance diversity is an essential component of Azerbaijan's foreign policy. To balance the influence of two
regional powers, Russia and Iran, Azerbaijan has always sought to build
strategic partnerships with allies beyond the Caucasus. Iran's rising
aggression, combined with Azerbaijan's interest in maintaining the status
quo balance of power in the South Caucasus, presents a strong impetus
to explore strategic alliance alternatives.

While relentlessly pursuing a policy of "revolution export," driven
by Tehran's desire to reverse its (self-inflicted) position of being an isolated state, Iran appears to be inciting subversive sectarianism in the
South Caucasus. The revisionist drive of Iran's regime and its aspirations to carve out a Shia "full moon"[327] underpin Tehran's re-intensified
attempts to manipulate the Shiite population in Azerbaijan, a country
which the Islamic Republic perceives as a historical part of the former
Persian Empire.

---

[327] Qais al-Khazali—leader of the Iraqi Shia militia, Asaib Ahl al-Haq (the League of the
Righteous, AAH)—announced that his organisation aims to establish a "Shiite full
moon not a Shiite crescent," and added "that an alliance of Shiite forces across the region
would be ready to achieve that goal by the time the hidden Shiite Imam Mahdi reap-
pears." For original quotations and brief analysis, see: Ahmad Majidyar, "Iran-Con-
trolled Militant Group Says Regional Alliance Will Create "Shiite Full Moon," *Middle
East Institute*, 11 May 2017, accessed 20 May 2018, http://www.mei.edu/content/io/iran
-controlled-militant-group-says-regional-alliance-will-create-shiite-full-moon.

The emerging strategic partnership with Saudi Arabia has the potential to develop into a potent alliance and to balance Iran's attempts to spread its political influence in Azerbaijan. From the perspective of international relations theory, both Azerbaijan and Saudi Arabia are status quo actors facing a revisionist threat¾Iran's attempts to alter the balance of power in the Middle East and South Caucasus. Both are targets of Iran's revisionist ambitions to build the "full moon," and both are threatened by the subversive activities of Tehran's proxies and attempts to radicalise and polarise their societies.

Although there are other common incentives behind the emerging strategic partnership between Azerbaijan and Saudi Arabia (including a mutual interest in diversification of their hydrocarbon-based economies), this chapter centres on Iranian expansionism. Iran's revisionist policy is analysed in the context of Azerbaijan's strategy of "overcoming geography," as well as its implications for both Azerbaijan and Saudi Arabia, respectively.

Azerbaijan's Foreign and Security Policy: Overcoming Geography

Positioned in a volatile part of the world, Azerbaijan is both a victim and benefactor of its geopolitical location.[328] Geopolitical factors form a cornerstone of Azerbaijan's domestic, foreign and security policies. As a relatively small state in this "dangerous region."[329] Azerbaijan has always designed its foreign and security policy based on realistic pragmatism and has chosen its allies from across the spectrum. Traditionally, Azerbaijan endeavours to maintain constructive relations with a variety of actors and, as a status quo advocate, strives to uphold the regional balance of power. Azerbaijan's Islamic heritage does not dictate its foreign policy. Instead, it practises flexibility in its choice of alliances—a vital factor which enables Azerbaijan to compensate for the challenges and limitations of its geopolitical settings.

Azerbaijan is positioned directly at the intersection of Eurasia's major energy and transport corridors. The politics of the region is

---

328 For a detailed account on history of Azerbaijan's political development, see for example: Suha Bolukbasi, *Azerbaijan: A Political History,* I. B. Tauris, 2013.

329 A theory developed by Mitchell A. Belfer in '*Small State, Dangerous Region: A Strategic Assessment of Bahrain,* Frankfurt: Peter Lang Publishers, 2014, 135–65.

predominantly shaped by the presence of natural resources, particularly in the Caspian Basin; the presence of three regional powers—Russia, Iran and Turkey; and the ongoing conflict between Azerbaijan and Armenia over Nagorno-Karabakh. Although its geopolitical location grants Azerbaijan direct access to energy resources in the Caspian Basin, the proximity of the three powers—all of them with ambitions to interfere in Azerbaijan's political sphere—presents a profound challenge to the country's sovereignty and security.[330]

Due to the geopolitics of the South Caucasus, and in particular the region's role as a transportation hub and hydrocarbon reservoir, Azerbaijan has been subject to external pressure ever since it gained independence from the USSR. Pressure has been exercised by exogenous actors such as the European Union and United States, as well as by local powers (Russia, Iran): all of them seeking to keep the post-Soviet republic in their spheres of influence.[331]

Neither Iran nor Russia welcomed Azerbaijan's decision to preserve its sovereignty, nor its determination to avoid becoming a proxy state of regional powers following independence in 1992. Instead, Azerbaijan has sought to minimise foreign influence in its political space. To secure and preserve Azerbaijan's primary national interest—sovereignty—Azerbaijan's government has had to adapt to realities of this "dangerous region."

Although Azerbaijan cannot be considered a classic small state, it is "relatively small" considering the immediate proximity of the great powers that surround it.[332] Like other "relatively small states" in dangerous regions, in order to ensure its survival and preserve its national interests, it is imperative that Azerbaijan's policy choices succeed in overcoming vulnerabilities stemming from its geopolitical configuration, and do not underestimate potential challenges.[333] The reality of being located in a "dangerous region" inevitably shapes Azerbaijan's decision-making process and both its foreign and domestic policies.

Since Azerbaijan seeks to maintain constructive relations with surrounding powers while simultaneously balancing their influence,

330 For a detailed account of Azerbaijan's geopolitics please see: Petersen, Alexandros & Fariz Ismailzade (eds.), *Azerbaijan in Global Politics: Crafting Foreign Policy*, Azerbaijan Diplomatic Academy, 2009.

331 "The South Caucasus Between Integration and Fragmentation", *Centre for Strategic Studies* (SAM), May 2015, accessed 25.04.2018, http://www.epc.eu/documents/uploads/pub_5598 _the_south_caucasus_-_low_res.pdf.

332 Belfer, *Small State, Dangerous Region*, 135–65.

333 Ibid., 130.

as a vital aspect of its foreign and security policy, the state has several, though limited, options to overcome its geopolitical vulnerability. According to Mitchell Belfer, there are three means by which Azerbaijan can overcome its geopolitical challenges: hegemony, neutrality, or alliance. In the case of Azerbaijan, the last of these—alliance—appears to be the preferable policy choice. In geopolitically sensitive regions, a functioning alliance produces a credible deterrence—which, in turn, helps to maintain the equilibrium of the status quo balance of power.[334] Hence, alliance-formation that generates credible deterrence is viewed as a vital mechanism to facilitate management of the inherent challenges which are associated with being a relatively small state in the dangerous region.

The spectrum of Azerbaijan's alliances is rather complex. Azerbaijan has pragmatically adopted a strategy of "alliance diversity," and thus refrains from being dependent on one power bloc or a single powerful ally.[335] In an attempt to limit the influence of its powerful neighbours, Azerbaijan has sought to build a network of alliances with states within and beyond the South Caucasus region. This diverse network of alliances forms the backbone of Azerbaijan's foreign policy and, to a great extent, Azerbaijan's national security is also determined by its alliance choices. Azerbaijan manoeuvres between West and East, oscillating between a range of diverse actors, and in so doing endeavours to maximise benefits granted by its strategic position, while minimising risks that stem from the destined geopolitical settings.[336] By ensuring diversity and balance in its alliance choices, Azerbaijan creates an effect of "soft deterrence," which allows the country to resist the influence of its powerful neighbours. Forging alliances with various (rival) actors often provides Azerbaijan with space to manoeuvre. Maintaining strong relations with powerful actors (including Russia, Turkey, Iran, Israel, the EU and United States) restricts other actors from direct, aggressive intervention in Azerbaijan's affairs—as long as the actor is unwilling to engage in a conflict with Azerbaijan's allies. Theoretically, such an alliance strategy pitches actors like Iran and Russia against each other, with each seeking to project influence over Azerbaijan. Yet, in fact, Azerbaijan benefits from

334 Mitchell A. Belfer, "Understanding Azerbaijan's Geopolitical Perceptions", *CEJISS*, 15 April 2015, accessed 05.06.2018, http://www.cejiss.org/editors-desk/understanding-azerbaijan-s-geopolitical-perceptions>.

335 Kamal Makili-Aliyev, "Azerbaijan's Foreign Policy: Between East and West", *IAI Working Papers* 13/05 – January 2013, 4-7.

336 Makili-Aliyev, "Azerbaijan's Foreign Policy", 4-7.

the existing rivalries between its allies. As Farhad Mammadov notes, "while the country tries to maintain the balance of power between the great nations in the region, it will also continue to benefit from the fact that these countries are in competition with each other for influence in the region.'[337]

Besides maintaining bilateral relations with both its regional neighbours and world powers, Azerbaijan has become a member of a great number of international organisations, such as the Commonwealth of Independent States (CIS), the Organization for Democracy and Economic Development (GUAM), the Parliamentary Assembly of the Council of Europe (PACE) and EU Eastern Partnership (EaP), the Organisation of Islamic Cooperation (OIC), the Black Sea Economic Cooperation (BSEC), the Economic Cooperation Organisation (ECO), and the Cooperation Council of Turkic Speaking States (CCTS).[338]

Thanks to Azerbaijan's strategy of alliance diversification, the country has managed to shape and secure a stable ground that allows it to avoid adopting political rules of engagement that are developed without its input. Azerbaijan continues to defend its national interest, despite being located in a "dangerous region" and surrounded by regional powers, all of which are keen to extend their influence over Azerbaijan and have a history of doing so.

The downside of Azerbaijan's alliance strategy is that it leaves the country's security relatively dependent on its allies and the credibility of their commitment. Azerbaijan thus is at constant risk of ally abandonment and must seek pre-emptively to prevent it. In this case, geopolitics work in Azerbaijan's favour. Its possession of large hydrocarbon reserves and the fact that Azerbaijan is located in the centre of the historical "Silk Road" trade routes makes Azerbaijan attractive to its allies. Azerbaijan is also positioned at the centre of the perpetual "Great Game" over Central Asia: "Azerbaijan's significant oil and gas reserves—hydrocarbon reserves are currently and rather modestly estimated at around 2.55 trillion cubic meters of gas and two billion tons of oil (while the predicted gas reserves of the country are estimated at six trillion cubic meters and oil reserves at four billion tons)—have allowed the country to develop more quickly

---

337 Farhad Mammadov, 'Azerbaijan's Foreign Policy – A New Paradigm of Careful Pragmatism", in *The South Caucasus Between Integration and Fragmentation*, *Centre for Strategic Studies* (SAM) May 2015, 29.
338 Mammadov, "Azerbaijan's Foreign Policy – A new Paradigm of Careful Pragmatism", 35.

than its neighbours and have been the cornerstone of its ties with the West."[339]

Last, but by no means least, despite its effective alliance strategy that minimises risks of direct and aggressive exogenous intervention, Azerbaijan is constantly threatened by more subtle means of foreign interference—social subversion, radical incitement, and "revolution export."

Common Incentive for Strategic Partnership: Status Quo Actors versus Revisionist Iran

The emerging strategic partnership between Saudi Arabia and Azerbaijan needs to be understood in the context of Iran's revisionist ambitions. While diplomatic relations between Azerbaijan and Saudi Arabia were established in 1992, when Saudi Arabia was among the first countries to recognise Azerbaijan's independence, it is Iran's aggressive expansionism which presents a common incentive for strategic partnership between the two states.

In the language of political science, both Azerbaijan and Saudi Arabia are defined as status quo actors.[340] As such, they are both targets of Iran's revisionist ambitions to build the "full moon." As the Islamic Republic—a chief revisionist in the Middle East and South Caucasus—strives to alter the regional balance of power in its favour, in order to become regional hegemon, both Azerbaijan and Saudi Arabia need to balance Iran's interference and its attempts to affect their respective foreign and domestic policies. At the centre of Tehran's revisionism is a desire to reverse its current position as a political "have-not"—an isolated Islamic revolutionary state.[341]

---

339 Mammadov, "Azerbaijan's Foreign Policy", 29.

340 Morgenthau declares that the policy of the status quo 'aims at the maintenance of the distribution of power that exists at a particular moment in history.' Hans J. Morgenthau, *Politics Among Nations: the Struggle for Power and Peace,* McGraw-Hill/Irwin, 1948 (2006 edition), 51.

341 Iran's revisionist nature, use of radical Islamic ideology and political violence, has earned it a definition of "R(I)RA": radical (Islamic) revisionist actor. RIRAs are *sui generis* political entities. A radical Islamic revisionist actor, RIRA, is defined as both state and pre-state (quasi state) entity whose raison d'être is anchored in a merger of revisionist political ideology and a radical Islamic ideology. Only such radical revisionist (non)-state actors whose ambition is to get control over an existing state, or to create a new one by territorial conquest, are classified RIRAs. In their revisionist struggle, RIRAs seek to gain monopoly over legitimate use of force, control public sphere and dictate both direction and character of the state's domestic and foreign policy. RIRAs view the establishment of a state entity as a stepping stone to challenge the established world order. RIRAs do not merely seek to alter socio-political order and become

Saudi support of Azerbaijan in the conflict with Armenia over Nagorno-Karabakh represents a manifestation of the polarisation between the two status quo advocates and revisionist Iran. The conflict itself is a historical precedent of the Islamic Republic's revisionist aspirations to weaken Azerbaijan and turn it into a satellite state. During the conflict, Iran has supported Armenia economically and turned a blind eye to the occupation of Azerbaijan's territory.[342] Contrary to Iran, Saudi Arabia has not established diplomatic relations with Armenia and has instead provided humanitarian and political support to Azerbaijan.

Recently, in response to Iran's intensified efforts to extend its influence over Azerbaijan, relations between Azerbaijan and Saudi Arabia have been developing in various spheres, including military, military-technology, and security. In February 2018, Saudi Minister of the Interior Prince Abdulaziz bin Saud Al Saud signed a protocol with Azerbaijan's Interior Minister Ramil Usubov for cooperation in the field of combating crime. Also in progress is a joint cooperation between the security services of both countries.[343] In July 2018, both states participated in Anatolia's Phoenix 2018 military drill, hosted by Turkey.[344] As part of an energy resources diversification strategy, which constitutes an essential element in both states' energy security, Azerbaijan and Saudi Arabia have expressed interest in developing synergy in the field of alternative energy. In March 2019, a memorandum of understanding was signed between the Azerbaijani Ministry of Energy and the Saudi Arabian company, ACWA Power. The document envisages that Azerbaijan and Saudi Arabia will cooperate in the field of renewable energy sources.[345]

---

the dominant ordering power within respective Westphalian nation-states. RIRAs aspire to defeat the Westphalian system and replace it. A study of radical (Islamic) revisionist actors (RIRAs) is a central subject of a doctoral thesis titled: "Origins of Radical Islamic Ideologies, Implications for Political Power-Struggles" conducted by Lucie Švejdová at the Metropolitan University Prague; the thesis defines and theorises RIRAs.

342 To learn more about Iran's stance during Nagorno-Karabakh, see, for example: Vusal Gasimli, Zaur Shiriyev, Zulfiyya Valiyeva, "Iranian-Armenian Relations, Geopolitical Reality versus Political Statements", *Center for Stategic Studies*, 2011.

343 "Cooperation Between Saudi Arabia, Azerbaijan in Combating Crime", *Asharq Al-Awsat*, 20 February 2018, accessed 23.04.2018, https://aawsat.com/english/home/article/1181411/cooperation -between-saudi-arabia-azerbaijan-combating-crime.

344 Sarp Ozer, "4-Nation Military Drill Launched in Central Turkey", *Anadolu Agency*, 1 July 2018, accessed 26.04.2018, https://www.aa.com.tr/en/turkey/4-nation-military-drill-launched -in-central-turkey/1192349.

345 "Azerbaijan, Saudi Arabia to Cooperate in Alternative Energy", *Azernews*, 17 March 2019, accessed 27.03.2019, https://www.azernews.az/oil_and_gas/147479.html.

Cooperation in the spheres of military and security is crucial, for both Saudi Arabia and Azerbaijan face subversive threats from Iran's proxies and attempts to radicalise and polarise their populations. To alter the regional balance of power and the political status quo in its favour, Iran has pursued a strategy of subversion and radical incitement. The notorious, repetitive pattern of the Islamic Republic's "revolution export" strategy is presented in the following comparison of Iran's attempts to influence Azerbaijan and Saudi Arabia, respectively.

Iran's Claims on Azerbaijan[346]

The bilateral relations between Azerbaijan and Iran have been complex, characterised by periodically escalating tensions, demographic and territorial challenges, as well as mutually beneficial and pragmatic cooperation. Iran has always claimed "natural" ownership over the Republic of Azerbaijan. This sense of entitlement is based on historical, demographic, religious, and geopolitical factors;[347] and it is also a component of Iran's revisionist strategy. In its quest to establish itself as a regional power, Iran uses the "empire" narrative and claims "natural ownership" of its former territories.

The first opportunity to turn Azerbaijan into its proxy was provided by the collapse of the Soviet Union in 1991, and the proximity of Iran has shaped Azerbaijan's foreign and security policies ever since. Once Azerbaijan freed itself from being one of the Soviet satellite states, Iran expected to consolidate its control over the newly independent republic.[348]

From a historical perspective, Iran viewed the collapse of the USSR as an opportunity to claim back the territory of today's Azerbaijan, which had been seized from the Qajar dynasty by the Russian Empire during the Russo-Persian Wars in the nineteenth century. Under the Treaty of

---

346 To read the original analysis of the bilateral relations between Azerbaijan and Iran, see: Lucie Švejdová, "Iran's Regional Ambitions: The Rising Power of Azerbaijan's Neighbour", *CEJISS* 11 (2), June 2017.

347 See for example: "Azerbaijan: Independent Islam And The State", *International Crisis Group Working to Prevent Conflict Worldwide,* Europe Report No. 191, 25 March 2008, 7-8; Houman A. Sadri, *Global Security Watch: The Caucasus States*, Westport: Praeger, 2010, 27-65; Dilip Hiro, *Inside Central Asia,* London: Duckworth, 2013, chapter 7.

348 Gallia Lenderstrauss and Iftah Celniker, "Azerbaijan and Iran: Hostile Approach but Limited Rivalry", *INSS Insight No. 366*, 26 August 2012, 1-2.

Turkmenchay in 1828, the Qajars completely surrendered their holdings in the South Caucasus, including parts of modern-day Azerbaijan and the Nakhchivan province.[349] After a brief period of independence between 1918 and 1920, Azerbaijan fell under the rule of the Soviet Union. Together with Armenia and Georgia, Azerbaijan became part of a political entity called the Transcaucasian Soviet Federative Socialist Republic, with all three later recognised as separate Soviet republic.[350]

Once the Soviet Union collapsed, Iran expected to fill the power vacuum and exploit its deep historical and cultural links with the South Caucasus.[351] Due to the strength of these ties (including the fact that Azerbaijan has a 96.9 percent Shia population),[352] from the Iranian perspective. Azerbaijan should have fallen effortlessly into its sphere of influence. In accordance with Article 11 of its constitution ("All Muslims are one nation. The Islamic Republic of Iran shall try to ensure political, economic and cultural unity of the Islamic world"[353]), Iran embarked on a strategy of "revolution export" in the South Caucasus. In the early 1990s, Iran launched a comprehensive program to expand its "Islamic Revolution" to the newly independent Caucasian states, including Azerbaijan. The programme was aimed at preventing the countries from adopting a pro-Western orientation, and the Islamic revival included the "export" of fundamentalist clerics and their teachings, as well as the creation of charity organisations.[354]

Despite Iran's efforts and expectations, and partially because the years of Soviet rule undermined the ties of Shia Islam between Azeris and Iranians, Azerbaijan decided to pursue independence and nationalism instead of accepting Iranian influence.[355] However, the demographic factors of Azerbaijan present a constant source of vulnerability. Since Azerbaijan's population is majority Turkic and Shia Muslim, the country's susceptibility to Iran's strategy of "revolution export" is relatively high. Despite the fact that the majority of Azerbaijan's population is

349 Sadri, *Global Security Watch: The Caucasus States,* 9.

350 Sadri, *Global Security Watch: The Caucasus States,* 31.

351 Vusal Gasimli, Zaur Shiriyev, Zulfiyya Valiyeva, 'Iranian-Armenian Relations, Geopolitical Reality versus Political Statements,' *Center for Stategic Studies* 2011, Baku, 4.

352 Data obtained from: CIA factbook, accessed 12.05.2018, https://www.cia.gov/library/publications /the-world-factbook/geos/aj.html.

353 The Constitution of the Islamic Republic of Iran, accessed 03.04.2018, https://www .constituteproject.org/constitution/Iran_1989.pdf?lang=en.

354 Alexander Murinson, "Iran Targets Azerbaijan", *BESA Center Perpsectives Paper No. 110,* 23 June 2010, accessed 16.04.2018, http://besacenter.org/perspectives-papers/iran-targets-azerbaijan/.

355 Sadri, *Global Security Watch: The Caucasus States,* 53-54.

secular, the cultural and religious ties still create favourable conditions for Iran to spread its ideology. Another aspect that makes Azerbaijan vulnerable to Iranian influence is that the large Azeri minority in Iran is highly integrated into the Islamic revolutionary elite; Iran's supreme leader Ayatollah Ali Khamene'i is Azeri, for instance.[356]

From the geopolitical perspective, probably one of the key sources of friction, and of Iranian desire to control Azerbaijan, is the division of natural resources in the Caspian Sea (including significant oil and natural gas deposits) between six countries: Russia, Azerbaijan, Kazakhstan, Turkmenistan, Uzbekistan, and Iran.[357] A tighter grip on Azerbaijan would naturally strengthen Iranian control over these resources.

Together, both demographic and geopolitical factors make Azerbaijan highly attractive in the eyes of the Islamic Republic. Theoretically, Iran perceives any instability within Azerbaijan as an opportunity to project its influence over its neighbour, with the ultimate goal of turning Azerbaijan into its proxy.

Despite a slight and brief change in Iran's approach towards Azerbaijan when Hassan Rouhani was elected President—contrary to the former administration of Ahmadinejad, Iran under Rouhani initially seemed less aggressive—the country has not relented, and on the contrary has increased, in its efforts to dominate Azerbaijan. Recently, Iran has intensified its attempts to manipulate Azerbaijan's Shiite population; a strategy that has been greatly facilitated by the informal lifting of a ban on preaching by foreign Islamic scholars.

Evidence is mounting that Iran is slowly increasing its capabilities in the country. According to Zaur Shiriyev, "Azerbaijan's government is growing increasingly concerned about what it sees as growing Iranian manipulation of the country's Shia Muslim believers."[358] Shiriyev continues that the decision in 2013 to relax restrictions on public preaching by religious figures linked to Iran appears to have had unintended consequences, resulting in increased control by Iran over Shia practice in Azerbaijan.[359]

---

356 Murinson, "Iran Targets Azerbaijan".

357 Visit: EIA, US Energy Information Administration; accessed 29.05.2018, http://www.eia.gov /todayinenergy/detail.cfm?id=12911

358 Zaur Shiriyev, "Azerbaijan Wrestles with Rising Iranian Influence", *Trackpersia*, 29 December 2017, accessed 27.05.2018, http://www.trackpersia.com/azerbaijan-wrestles-rising-iranian-influence.

359 Shiriyev, "Azerbaijan Wrestles with Rising Iranian Influence". See also: Huda al-Husseini, "Will Iran turn Azerbaijan into Another Iraq?", *Al Arabiya English*, 26 January 2018,

Farhad Mammadov draws attention to the proliferation of religious fanaticism in Azerbaijan, which he perceives as being caused by strengthening Iranian influence in the region.[360] The massive increase in the number of people participating in the Ashura ceremonies in September 2017—where the predominantly secular Azerbaijanis were shocked to see children participating in rituals including self-flagellation—is believed to demonstrate Iran's increased control of Azerbaijan's population. The MP Zahid Oruc commented: "When I saw children, who do not have a real understanding of religion, wearing hijab and attending Ashura ceremonies, I thought they are going to become kamikazes to be sent in the future to Syria."[361]

Mammadov further notes that, along with the massive growth in the number of believers participating in the Ashura ceremonies, the number of pilgrims to Karbala also increased dramatically. According to the statistics of travel agencies that organise tours to the sacred site in Iran, in 2017 there was a 33 percent increase in Azerbaijanis visiting Karbala compared to the previous year. Interestingly, it is Iran's Islamic Revolutionary Guard Corps (IRGC)—which is notorious for training radical militias across the Middle East—and its associated Shiite militia *Hashdi Shabi*, which undertake to ensure the protection of pilgrims. It is believed that pilgrims have been exposed to radical incitement against Azerbaijan's government, particularly focusing on Nardaran, the centre of a conservative Shiite population which had been similarly targeted by Iran in the past.[362]

These examples imply that Iran has re-intensified its efforts to "export Iranian Islamic revolution" to Azerbaijan by proliferating radicalism amongst the population and thus encouraging insurgency against the established government. This same strategy has been used by the Islamic Republic across the Middle East—including in the Kingdom of Saudi Arabia.

---

accessed 27.05.2018, https:/english.alarabiya.net/en/views/news/middle-east/2018/01/26/Will-Iran-turn-Azerbaijan-into-another-Iraq-.html.

360 Farhad Mammadov, "Iran vtorgayetsa v Azerbaydzhan oruzhiyem palomnikov", *Haqqin.az,* 1 December 2017, accessed 26.05.2018, https://haqqin.az/news/117537.

361 Quoted in: *QMİ:* "Ushaq Ashura gunu meschide gedirse, bu chokh gozel haldir", 3 October 2017, accessed 15.05.2018, accessed 27.05.2018, https://www.azadliq.org/a/ashura-ushaq-hicab/28771372.html.

362 Farhad Mammadov, "Iran vtorgayetsa v Azerbaydzhan oruzhiyem palomnikov", Haqqin, 1 December 2017, available: https://haqqin.az/news/117537; Shiriyev, "Azerbaijan Wrestles with Rising Iranian Influence".

Subversion in Saudi Arabia

The Islamic Republic of Iran has dragged Saudi Arabia into a long-standing proxy war. As political turmoil continues in Syria, Iraq, and Yemen, Iran has clearly abandoned its Shia crescent for a "full moon" approach, leading it to recruit, support, finance, and train numerous proxy groups and to place them into strategic positions. These Shia paramilitary groups serve as enforcers of the Islamic Republic, to tilt the balance of power in the Middle East in Tehran's favour and to realise the Ayatollahs' revisionist dream of taking a leading role in the region and replacing Saudi Arabia as the custodian of Islam.

Iran often equates battlefield "victory" in one location with steps towards victories in others. From this perspective, the subversive activities of Iran-backed militias in Yemen, Bahrain, Lebanon, Iraq, and Syria are viewed as stepping stones to gaining influence over Saudi Arabia. As Iran deliberately destabilises adjacent countries and restrains their high command, it establishes logistical routes for its agents. These strategic axes—particularly those in the Arab Gulf—then serve as staging grounds to harass Saudi Arabia.

In Yemen, for example, Tehran's strategic interest is to extend the ongoing conflict across the border into Saudi territory, and it is well documented that the Islamic Republic provides Yemen's Houthi paramilitaries not only with weaponry and expertise, but also with military supervision. Already in early 2015, Iranian parliamentarian Ali Reza Zakani publicly revealed these intentions when he stated that "the Yemeni revolution [...] will be extended [...] to Saudi territory and [...] the people of the Eastern Province of Saudi Arabia will lead those protests."[364]

From their safe haven in Yemen, Iran-backed militias also raid Saudi oil facilities, in order to damage the Saudi economy. Installations of Saudi Arabian Oil Co. have been attacked multiple times since March 2018. Vital hydrocarbon transportation routes are also in danger of disruption. In January 2018, Houthi militias threatened to block the strategic Red Sea shipping lane, an important trade route for oil tankers, which pass

---

[363] For the original analysis and full research series on Iran's regional subversion read: Lucie Švejdová, "Mapping Militias in the Middle East", *EGIC,* 2018; accessed 16.08.2018, https://www.egic.info/gulf-bulletins.

[364] Quoted by Lori Plotkin Boghardt, in "Gulf Fears of Iranian Subversion", *The Washington Institute for Near East Policy,* 2 April 2015, accessed 18.07.2018, http://www.washingtoninstitute.org/policy-analysis/view/gulf-fears-of-iranian-subversion.

proximate to Yemeni shores while heading from the Middle East through the Suez Canal to Europe.[365]

Moreover, as in the case of Azerbaijan, Iran strives to undermine Saudi Arabia from within. To do so, Iran fuels a negative Shia–Sunni dichotomy and seeks to antagonise Saudi's Shia population. Tehran has attempted to alienate and segregate the Shia population of the Eastern Province from the rest of the country, through the calculated instigation of sectarian violence. Agents of the Islamic Republic, such as Hezbollah Al-Hejaz, are known to infiltrate the local Shia minority and supply it with munitions and military equipment in large numbers. on the flimsy pretext of "defending the Shia community from the Saud." Through deliberate radicalisation and armament of fractions of the Shia population, Iran seeks to ignite armed insurrection that would justify Iranian military intervention against the Kingdom.

In its quest to destabilise and ultimately overthrow the Saudi government, Iran collaborates with (Sunni) jihadi groups and follows a "strategic and tactical flexibility" approach. Of particular concern are Tehran's fluid and long-lasting links with al-Qaeda (and parts of ISIS). This "marriage of convenience,"[366] which dates back at least a quarter of a century, was exposed in the 9/11 Commission Report.[367] The report revealed that senior al-Qaeda figures maintained close ties to Iranian security officials and had frequently travelled across Iran's border—including at least eight of the fourteen operatives selected for the 9/11 attacks.[368] In 2007, Osama bin Laden himself acknowledged the murky relations between Iran and al-Qaeda, by referring to Iran as al-Qaeda's "main artery for funds, personnel and communication."[369]

The nature of the relationship between Iran and al-Qaeda is best defined as "tactical cooperation." As Assaf Moghadam notes, tactical cooperation is not necessarily based on ideological affinity, and the actors engaged in a tactical alliance tend to maintain their organisational

---

365 For full report see: Aziz El Yaakoubi, "Yemen's Houthis Threaten to Block Red Sea Shipping Lane", *Reuters*, 9 January 2018, accessed 07.05.2018, https://www.reuters.com/article/us-yemen-security/yemens-houthis-threaten-to-block-red-sea-shipping-lane-idUSKBN1EY2AP.

366 Assaf Moghadam, "Marriage of Convenience: The Evolution of Iran and al-Qa'ida's Tactical Cooperation", *CTC Sentinel*, April 2017.

367 The full document is available at: http://govinfo.library.unt.edu/911/report/911Report.pdf.

368 See Greg Bruno, "State Sponsors: Iran," *Council on Foreign Relations*, updated 13 October 2011, accessed 14.05.2018, https://www.cfr.org/backgrounder/state-sponsors-iran.

369 Quoted by Iman Zayat, "When Hamza bin Laden Stumbles and Falls in Line with Iran", *The Arab Weekly*, 8 April 2018, accessed 24.05.2018, https://thearabweekly.com/when-hamza-bin-laden-stumbles-and-falls-line-iran.

independence. Rather than based on mutual trust, tactical cooperation is conditioned by the perception of common interests, such as the identification of a common enemy. Following 9/11, Iran provided safe passage to many members of al-Qaeda, including the group's senior members and their families.[370] Despite Tehran's denials, Iran has sheltered al-Qaeda operatives (including Hamza bin Laden, the son of Osama who was seen as the emerging leader of the terrorist organisation) and allowed them to use Iran as a hub for their activities.

Conclusion

The emerging strategic partnership between Azerbaijan and Saudi Arabia needs to be understood in the context of Iran's regional revisionist ambitions. As status quo advocates, both Azerbaijan and Saudi Arabia face a revisionist threat from the Islamic Republic. This common security challenge provides a strong incentive to intensify their mutual strategic cooperation.

For Azerbaijan, the rising aggression of Iran's attempts to interfere in its political affairs and to manipulate its population presents a clear security threat. After the lifting of the informal ban on foreign Islamic preachers, Iran's capability to export revolution—to ignite radicalism that might lead to anti-government insurgency—has significantly increased. Iran may embrace this opportunity to breed subversion by following the same pattern that has proved successful in the Middle East, most notably in Yemen, Syria, Iraq, Lebanon, Bahrain, and Saudi Arabia. Apart from radical incitement, the potential security risks might also involve Iran's support for an assortment of paramilitaries. Following Tehran's modus operandi in the Middle East, these terrorist groups might receive training in Iranian camps under the patronage of organisations such as the Islamic Revolutionary Guard Corps and Hezbollah, in order to operate on Azerbaijani terroritory with the purpose of undermining stability of its government.

The strengthening of the alliance between Azerbaijan and Saudi Arabia, both targets of Iran's policy of revolution export, provides an opportunity to exchange intelligence, particularly in the sphere of counterterrorism related to Iranian expansion. The formation of an alliance

---

370 Moghadam, "Marriage of Convenience", 13.

bloc, consisting of status quo advocates, holds potential for the creation of a credible deterrence which might increase Azerbaijan's chances of preventing the spread of Iranian influence in Azerbaijan and the wider South Caucasus.

AUTHORS

Shamkhal Abilov is a lecturer in the International Relations department of Baku Engineering University and a PhD Candidate at Humboldt University in Berlin. Abilov's research interests include Azerbaijan, Conflict Studies, Caspian Studies (Caucasus and Central Asia), as well as Urban Studies, ethnicity, and nationalism. Abilov is the author of various academic articles related to his research interests.

Mitchell Belfer is a specialist in geopolitics and security in Europe, the wider Middle East and the Caucasus region. Belfer founded the Department of International Relations and European Studies (2006) and the Central European Journal of International and Security Studies (2007) at the Metropolitan University Prague. His current position is President of the Euro-Gulf Information Centre in Rome, Italy (2015-present). In addition to the wide range of scholarly works Belfer has authored, he is also a frequent commentator in the international press and has appeared on the BBC, CNN, and Radio France International. Belfer sits on the boards of many important scientific organizations in Europe and the Middle East; he has recently joined the editorial board of the International Journal of Humanitarian Studies. Belfer's current focus is on asymmetric warfare and political radicalisation.

Robert M. Cutler is a fellow of the Canadian Global Affairs Institute, a practitioner member of the University of Waterloo's Institute for Complexity and Innovation, and senior research fellow and director of the NATO Association of Canada's Energy Security Program. Educated at MIT, with a doctorate from the University of Michigan, he has published widely on energy geoeconomics in Europe and Eurasia, as well as advising governments, international institutions, and the private sector on energy project development for over two decades.

Kamran Ismayilov holds a doctoral degree in International Relations from the Scuola Superiore Sant'Anna in Pisa, Italy. His research interests concern EU–Russian relations, as well as their foreign policy initiatives relating to their mutual neighbouring countries. In the past, Ismayilov has conducted research on the South Caucasus and taken part in multi-partner projects and conferences relating to Post-Soviet Studies

Farid Shafiyev is a diplomat and scholar from Azerbaijan, chairman of the Baku-based Centre of Analysis of International Relations, and former Ambassador of Azerbaijan to Canada and the Czech Republic. He holds a PhD from Carleton University and an MPA from Harvard Kennedy School of Government, as well as a Bachelor of Law and Diploma in History from Baku State University. He is the author of *Resettling the Borderlands: State Relocations and Ethnic Conflict in the South Caucasus* (McGill-Queen's University Press, 2018) and numerous articles and op-eds.

Lucie Švejdová is currently a PhD Candidate at the Metropolitan University Prague. In her research, she focuses on politics of the wider Middle East, security, counterterrorism, and radical ideologies.

Anar Valiyev is associate professor at ADA University. He received his Bachelor's degree in History (1999) and a Master's degree in History (2001), both from Baku State University. From 2001 to 2003, he studied public policy at the School of Public and Environmental Affairs at Indiana University in Bloomington, where he received his second Master's. In 2007, he successfully defended his doctoral dissertation at the School of Urban and Public Affairs at the University of Louisville, Kentucky. From 2007 to 2008, he worked as assistant professor at Masaryk University in the Czech Republic, and in 2016–2017 he was a Fulbright Visiting Scholar at Johns Hopkins University.

INDEX